Crickhowell Castle

THE CASTLES
OF MID WALES
Mike Salter

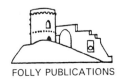

FOLLY PUBLICATIONS

ACKNOWLEDGEMENTS

The photographs in this book were taken by the author. He also drew the map and the plans, which are on common scales of 1:400 for keeps, etc, 1:800 for courtyards, and 1:2000 for earthworks and large sites. Thanks to Max Barfield, who did the driving for some of the fieldwork for this book in the first half of 1991, and also to Gwyn Evans of Brecon who provided a copy of the print of Pencelli Castle.

AUTHOR'S NOTES

This series of books (see full list inside the back cover) are intended as portable field guides giving as much informationn and illustrative material as possible in volumes of modest size, weight and price. As a whole the series aims to make information available about less well known buildings. The aim in the castle books has been to mention, where the information is known to the author, owners or custodians of buildings who erected or altered parts of them, and those who were the first or last of a line to hold an estate, an important office, or a title. Those in occupation at the time of dramatic events such as sieges are also often named. Other owners and occupants whose lives had little effect on the condition of the buildings are generally not mentioned, nor are ghost stories, myths and legends.

The books are intended to be used in conjunction with the Ordnance Survey 1:50,000 scale maps. Grid references are given in the gazetteers together with a coded system indicating which buildings can be visited or easily seen by the public from adjacent open spaces which is explained on page 72. An Ordnance Survey map is essential for finding the majority of the sites described in this book.

Each level of a building is called a storey in this book, the basement being the first storey with its floor near courtyard level unless specifically mentioned as otherwise.

Measurements given in the text and scales on the plans are in metres, the unit used by the author for all measurements taken on site. Although the buildings were designed using feet and inches the metric scales are much easier to use and are noiw standard amongst academics working on historic buildings and ancient sites. Unless specifically mentioned as otherwise all dimensions are external at or near ground level, but above the plinth if there is one. On the plans the original work is shown black, post 1800 work is stippled and alterations and additions of intermediate periods are hatched. Because of the nature of earthworks all dimensions referring to them given in the text are only approximate to the nearest metre.

ABOUT THE AUTHOR

Mike Salter is 47 and has been a professional writer and publisher since he went on the Government Enterprise Allowance Scheme for unemployed people in 1988. He is particularly interested in the planning and layout of medieval buildings and has a huge collection of plans of churches and castles he has measured during tours (mostly by bicycle and motorcycle) throughout all parts of the British Isles since 1968. Wolverhampton born and bred, Mike now lives in an old cottage beside the Malvern Hills. His other interests include walking, maps, railways, board games, morris dancing, playing percussion instruments and calling dances with a folk group.

Dolforwyn Castle

CONTENTS

Inside the front cover is a map of sites described in this book.

INTRODUCTION

The type of defensible lordly residence which the Normans called a castle was unknown in Wales until they invaded that country in the late 11th century. The Normans had evolved a class of building usually having a stone or timber tower acting as a citadel, a secure dwelling for the owner, and as a status symbol. Such citadels were not found in the forts built by Welsh princes and chieftains hitherto, nor in the forts constructed by the Romans. Norman courtiers of the penultimate Saxon King of England, Edward the Confessor, built three castles in Herefordshire in the 1050s and after the invasion of England in 1066 they were built in profusion throughout the country, proving an effective means of keeping the Saxons subjugated. The Normans also used a system called feudalism under which great lords held land from the king in return for military service and they in turn let knights hold land from them in return for specified annual periods of military service, which often took the form of garrison duty at a castle.

The early Norman kings of England formed a barrier against the Welsh by creating marcher lordships whose holders were allowed to have more compact groups of manors than elsewhere, resulting in the concentrated military strength needed to hold the Welsh at bay. As they had their own judicial system the Marcher lords effectively became petty kings themselves. Before long these lords became strong enough to occasionally challenge the might of the English crown, yet it was not until 1536 that they were finally abolished by Henry VIII. Shropshire and Herefordshire then assumed their present shape whilst the counties of Brecon (then called Brecknock), Radnor and Montgomery were created. These three counties, offically united in 1974 to form the new county of Powys, form the subject area of this book.

William I (The Conqueror) and his successor William II (Rufus) allowed the Marcher lords to make whatever progress they could in occupying Wales, which was then ruled by three major princes, Gwynedd, Deheubarth, and Powys, plus a number of lesser independent rulers. Welsh custom divided property equally among all sons and allowed any adult male close relative to claim the title of a deceased ruler. This led to perpetual family squabbles and military and economic weakness which the Normans were able to exploit. In the 1070s Roger de Montgomery, named after Montgomerie in Normandy, built a castle then called Montgomery but now known as Hen Domen. Two other castles in the Severn Valley are likely to be relics of his advances into Welsh territory in the 1080s, whilst it is just possible that Castell Dinas, high above Talgarth, is also of this period.

The motte near the church at Hay-on-Wye

The motte of Builth Castle

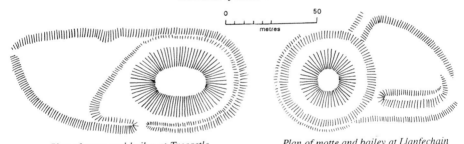

Plan of motte and bailey at Trecastle *Plan of motte and bailey at Llanfechain*

In 1093 the Normans made a major breakthrough when Bernard de Newmarch defeated and killed Rhys ap Tewdwr, ruler of Deheubarth, and captured Gwrgan ap Bleddyn, ruler of Brycheiniog. The battle took place near Brecon, where Bernard immediately built a castle to consolidate his victory. His followers soon built chains of castles along the river valleys, notably Aberllynfi, Hay and Bronllys beside the Wye, and Pencelli, Tretower and Crickhowell along the Usk. Ralph Mortimer advanced from Wigmore Castle to take Elfael and Maelienydd from the Welsh. He or his followers built the castles of Radnor, Knighton, Gemaron and Cefnllys. Shortly after this Payn Fitz-John built Painscastle in Radnorshire and Philip de Braose created a lordship of Buellt (Builth) based on a castle at Caer Beris.

The Welsh soon contested the Norman territorial gains. In 1094 Roger de Newburgh had to rescue Bernard de Mewmarch from a Welsh blockade around Brecon Castle. That castle held out against the Welsh on several occasions, except perhaps in the 1260s. Other castles such as Builth, Gamaron, and Cefnllys were repeatedly destroyed and rebuilt over the next two centuries, being captured when the Welsh were temporarily united under strong leaders and the Normans were weak, like during the period of anarchy during King Stephen's reign (1136-54). As soon as the Normans recovered the castle site were reoccupied and their defences rebuilt. Eventually the Welsh began to build castles themselves, the earliest instance of this probably being that at Welshpool erected in 1111 by the Prince of Powys.

The early castles in Mid Wales were rarely of mortared stone in their original form. Instead they were mostly built of earth and wood, more suitable materials for cheap and quick construction work by gangs of slave labour. A common form comprised an earth mound or motte surmounted by a timber tower or house with a small palisaded court around it. A bailey or base court at a lower level to one side contained a hall, chapel, workshops, stables, granary, and a range of other farm buildings, protected by a palisade set on a rampart formed by digging a ditch in front of it. All the buildings would be timber framed with wattle and daub often used to fill in the panels between the posts. The tower on the mound formed a private dwelling for the lord and a last refuge if the weaker bailey defences should succumb to an attack. The basic design was varied at each site according to the terrain, labour, and time available. What is now known as a ringwork, which is an enclosure with a high bank, might replace the motte, whilst baileys were omitted or duplicated or laid out to whatever shape and size the terrain was suitable for and depending on the number out outbuildings required. Castles forming the admistrative centres of major lordships quite often had at least two baileys of some size in addition to a keep and outworks defending the gateways. An outer bank or counterscarp often lay behind the main ditch and occasionally there is a second ditch beyond that. Natural spurs and hillocks were utilised where possible, being scarped into steep-sided mottes with (more or less) level summits. Over a hundred earthworks of these various types dating from the 1070s to the 1190s remain in Mid Wales, good examples being Builth, Hen Domen, Gro Tump, Llanfechain, Painscastle, Rhos Ddiarbed and Trecastle.

Stone blocks were occasionally used as the cores of mottes and small buildings were sometimes crudely erected with drystone walling, but walls properly constructed with mortar and dressed stone openings required considerable capital, numerous craftsmen, and several years of fairly peaceful conditions for their construction. In the area covered by this book the earliest standing masonry wals for which a fairly secure date can be suggested is the shell wall built to enclose the small low mound at Tretower c1160. Typical round-arched Norman windows with small external openings and wide internal splays survive in the parts of the shell wall which had two storey domestic blocks built against it to contain a hall and a private room or solar for the lord. There was also a small square projecting tower to contain the gateway. The more important castle at Brecon may have gained its shell keep about the same period, but it lacks datable features. Other shell walls (now reduced to buried footings) on mounds at Symon's Castle and Crickhowell are probably later. The substantial square tower keep at Pencelli and the smaller rectangular towers at Bleddfa and Hyssington may have existed by the 1190s. Two other keeps, the tiny much altered tower at Hay, and the larger building at Dinas, now mostly buried in its own rubble, are probably earlier and could go back to the late 11th century. These keeps would each contain a dark cellar at ground level reached only by a trap-door from the hall or main living room above, the entrance into which was reached by an external timber stair. A third storey, if there was one, would contain a bedroom. A typical Norman window survives at Hay, where the curtain wall with its surviving gateway arch may also be of the end of the 12th century. At Castell Dinas the keep had the unusual feature of a low chemise wall set closely around it. An inner ward adjoins it with square flanking towers, and then there is a large outer ward. Several other sites, such as Clyro, traces of walls likely to be of 12th century date but there is no means of dating these works accurately without systematic exacation. The only contemporary written record of construction work likely to concern masonry at any of the castles in Mid Wales during the 12th century refers to the now-vanished wall built in 1194 around the bailey at Carreghofa.

The Fitz Herberts are thought to have built a new stone castle at Blaenllynfi c1208-15 in preference to wind-swept Castell Dinas. The erection of a new stone castle at Montgomery by Henry III in the 1220s to replace Hen Domen heralded a spate of replacements of timber defences at older sites by stone walls. The new castle had a small but strong inner ward with a large D-shaped tower on one side, a smaller tower at the far end, and was entered through a gatehouse fronted by two round towers. The gatehouse upper storeys formed the main hall and private chamber. In the 1230s Henry III built a curtain wall with towers and a gatehouse and a circular tower keep on the motte at Pain's Castle, and he repaired recent damage done to Hay Castle. At about the same time the Picard family erected a circular tower keep and curtain walls with round corner towers at Tretower, and the Cliffords built a keep and possibly also a curtain wall at Bronllys. In the 1240s King Henry had the castle at Builth rebuilt in stone, and he walled in the middle ward at Montgomery, whilst the Mortimer family erected a new castle at Cefnllys and strengthened Blaenllynfi. It may have been about the same time that a curtain wall with a gatehouse was built at Brecon by the de Bohun earl of Hereford, whilst the curtain wall at the nearby palace of the bishop of St Davids may also be of this period.

Thomas Corbet began the erection of a square court with corner towers on a rock at Nantcribba in the 1260s but during that decade the Norman castles of Mid Wales probably saw more buildings demolished than erected. Llywelyn ap Gruffydd took advantage of the civil war raging between Henry III and Simon de Montfort to capture and destroy many of the Mortimer castles in Maelienydd and Elfael, and to occupy the district around the de Bohun seat at Brecon. Probably erected by the Welsh during this period was the small pentagonal court at Castell Coch with a possibly older rectangular keep and one large round tower, both probably of just two storeys. Llywelyn is recorded as having built the castle at Dolforwyn to assert his authority in Powys and defy Henry III, whose own castle of Montgomery lies not far away. Dolforwyn also has a round tower at one end and a rectangular keep (again possibly older) at the other, together with three ranges of apartments and a U-shaped tower.

Window in the keep at Bronllys

The gateway at Hay Castle

The embattled show front of Tretower Court

In the 1270s the Mortimers refortified Cefnllys, Tinboeth and Pencelli, whilst the isolated round keep at Cwm Camlais was either Welsh work or an outpost of the de Bohuns. Several other sites looking like mottes could be the lower parts of round towers buried in their own debris. Cefnllys had a round or octagonal keep within a small square court with round corner towers. Tinboeth was an oval without flanking towers although there was a gatehouse with twin round-fronted towers flanking the passageway like that which survived at Pencelli until at least the mid 18th century.

Edward I (1272-1307) carried out some remodelling at Montgomery and then in 1277, as part of his campaign against Llewelyn ap Gruffydd, began rebuilding Builth Castle with a circular keep on the motte and a curtain wall with six D-shaped towers and a gatehouse. The gatehouse, at least, was left incomplete after Llywelyn was killed in a skirmish nearby in December 1282. Although there were one or two minor later revolts, no other ruler then managed to unite the Welsh for over a hundred years, thus reducing the need for strong (and expensive) new fortifications. In the 1280s the castle at Crickhowell was rebuilt in stone and at Aberedw the motte was abandoned and a new stone castle with a square courtyard with circular corner towers erected further east. Around 1300 the de Bohuns built a new hall block at Brecon, now the only domestic building surviving in a recognisable state amongst any of the castles in Mid Wales, except for a still more ruined building of uncertain date at Llanddew. At Powys the former princes seem to have erected a square keep and separate hall block c1280-1300, to which their successors the Charltons in the first half of the 14th century added a massive pair of large round towers on either side of the inner gate and added an outer ward with further round towers. The much altered square towers at Scethrog and Talgarth could be of almost any period between the early 13th and mid 14th centuries. As far as is known, these buildings stood alone without outworks or outbuildings of importance, except for a wet moat at Scethrog.

Holes over gateway at Tretower

There is both documentary and archaeological evidence of timber buildings on motte and bailey castles being maintained until the late 13th century and occasionally into the 14th century. Pudding-shaped mottes all seem to be of c1075-1175, but other earthwork types were sometimes built in later periods. Hubert de Burgh began a ringwork in Kerry Woods in 1228 and in the 1280s the newly founded towns beside the River Severn at Llanidloes and Newtown were each given a large but low mound with timber buildings protecting the side of the settlement away from the river and thus more exposed to attack. Another type only occasionally found in central Wales is the quadrangular water-filled moat around a platform 30m to 60m long. These mark the sites of manor houses and rectories not otherwise fortified, except for that at Hen Castell which had a curtain wall. It may be earlier than the other sites of this type, which probably date from after the Welsh threat was lessened with Llywelyn ap Gryffudd's death in 1282, although moated platforms appeared earlier in the 13th century in England. Water-filled ditches were not necessarily military in purpose. A moat was a permanent and efficient boundary for keeping vagrants, wild animals and malefactors out of manorial enclosures, and would have been equally useful for controlling the comings and goings of domestic animals, servants and members of the owner's family. At all periods moats have been appreciated as scenic features and they served as a habitat for fish, eels, and water fowl which together formed a substantial part of the diet of the landed classes. A wet moat could also help to drain land otherwise unsuitable for agriculture or inhabitation.

In the medieval period castle walls of rubble were usually limewashed outside to make them watertight, making them look very different to the way they do today. Dressed (cut) stones around windows and doorways would be left uncovered. Domestic rooms would have had whitewashed walls perhaps decorated with murals of biblical, historical or heroic scenes mostly painted in yellow and black. However, less money was probably spent on elaborating the rooms in vulnerable remote strongholds than in the more peaceful parts of England. Wall hangings decorated with the same themes or heraldry gradually into use from the 14th century onwards. Although used in churches, glass was expensive and uncommon in secular buildings before the 15th century, so windows were originally closed with wooden shutters. No examples of this remain in central Wales but shutters remain in the halls of the Shropshire castles of Ludlow and Stokesay. The rooms were dark when the weather was too cold or wet for the shutters to be opened for light and ventilation. Large openings in the outer walls sometimes had iron stanchions in them, even if quite high above the ground. Living rooms usually had fireplaces although some halls had central hearths with the smoke escaping through louvres in the roof. Latrines squeezed into the thickness of the walls were common, but few now survive in Mid Wales castles.

Furnishings were sparse up until the 15th century, although the embrasures of upper storey windows often have built-in stone seats, as at Bronllys. Lords with several castles tended to circulate around them, administering their manorial courts and consuming agricultural produce on the spot, although in practice they might often be attendant upon the king anywhere in England, or engaged on military or diplomatic service far from the Welsh Marches. Seats belonging to great lords could be left almost empty when they were not in residence, although castles in the Welsh Marches were garrisoned almost continuously until the end of the 13th century, after which they only tended to be manned in times of unrest. Servants travelled with lords and sometimes also portable furnishings such as rugs, wall hangings, cooking vessels and bedding, all kept in wooden chests. The lord and his immediate family plus honoured guests and the senior household officials would enjoy a fair degree of privacy, having their own rooms. Servants and retainers enjoyed less comfort and privacy, sharing of beds and communal sleeping in the main hall and warm places of work like the kitchen and stables being common.

Roger Mortimer of Wigmore briefly ruled England and Wales along with his lover Queen Isabella after they deposed her husband Edward II in 1326. Roger was created Earl of March but was executed when the teenage Edward III declared himself old enough to govern in 1330. The 2nd earl of March repaired the castles of Montgomery and Bronllys in the 1360s but on the whole the castles were neglected during the 14th century, which was a comparatively peaceful period for central Wales. They were repaired and garrisoned against Owain Glyndwr, who was in revolt against Henry IV for the first dozen years of the 15th century, and some of them were captured by the rebels. In 1424 the Mortimer estates passed by marriage to Richard, Earl of Cambridge, who became Duke of York in 1426. He had little use for remote crumbling border strongholds, although Cefnllys seems to have been maintained until the Duke was killed fighting the Lancastrians at Wakefield in 1460. His son took the throne in 1461 as Edward IV, ruling until 1483. The Dukes of Stafford inherited the castles of Brecon and Hay, which they kept in repair, and Bronllys, which was allowed to decay. Powis Castle was divided between heiresses resulting in the Greys inhabiting and maintaining the inner ward whilst the Suttons, whose chief seat was Dudley Castle in Staffordshire, allowed the ranges in the outer ward to decay. The conflicts of 1455 to 1485 left the castles of central Wales unaffected. At Tretower the Bluets and their successors the Vaughans were content to live in an undefended manor house within sight of the crumbling old castle. The Vaughans did add a gatehouse and an embattled wall with arrow loops on one side of the house in the 1490s but these seem to have been to impress visitors rather than for defence since the other sides of the house lacked any defensive features. They built a similar gatehouse at Great Porthaml and the Herberts built another at their house of Cwrt Y Carw at Crickhowell.

In the 1530s the gatehouse at New Radnor was patched up for use as a county gaol, and Montgomery Castle was repaired for use as a military and administrative centre. The great hall at Brecon used for county court sessions was re-roofed during this period. New mansions were built in the courtyards at Pencelli in the 1580s, Montgomery in the 1620s, and Hay in 1660s. The castles of Brecon, New Radnor and Powis were captured and slighted by Parliamentary troops during the Civil War of the 1640s, whilst the castle at Montgomery was slighted without having to withstand a siege.

Not much now remains of the fabric of most of the castles of Mid Wales. They were mostly built of shale with rendering required to keep the walls watertight. Shale fractures very easily and after long periods of neglect most of the castles became just piles of fallen rubble which either became buried under earth and vegetation or were taken away for reuse elsewhere. The stone castles of Radnorshire in particular are mostly reduced to buried footings still awaiting uncovering by archaeologists. Montgomeryshire has Powis Castle surviving complete and fully furnished but much altered from its medieval state, whilst the lower parts of Montgomery and Dolforwyn have been exposed by the Welsh Office and their successor Cadw. Brecon has more to be seen, since the much altered tower houses of Scethrog and Talgarth remain roofed and there are ruins still remaining at Brecon, Blaenllynfi, Hay, Llanddew, Bronllys and Crickhowell, with free access to the last three. Other remains are of a more minor nature, although there is a fair bit to see at Castell Dinas. Buildings such as the gatehouse at Pencelli and the hall block at Bronllys survived until the mid 18th century, late enough to be shown on old engravings and paintings, and recorded in the site descriptions left to us by antiquarians and tourists of that period.

GAZETTEER OF CASTLES IN BRECONSHIRE

ABERLLYNFI CASTLE   SO 171380

A natural platform about 48m long by 30m wide which rises 4m above what was formerly marshland forms a bailey presumably once divided from the level ground to the east by a ditch. A mound 2m high with a summit 15m across lying at the west end, where there is a stream, may actually be the buried base of a circular stone keep. The castle is mentioned in documents of the period 1180-1211 and in September 1233 was given by Henry III to Inges, one of his crossbowmen. The castle was recovered shortly afterwards by Hugh Kinnersley, the original owner, and fortified on behalf of his overlord Walter de Clifford, who was then in rebellion. King Henry then ordered Henry de Turbeville to recapture the castle. The platform with a 3m deep rock cut ditch 0.3km to the east could be a siegework of this period.

ABERYSCIR CASTLE   SO 000296

A motte lies in trees above the junction of the Usk and Afon Yscir. A ditch protects the approach from the north. The summit measures 30m by 20m and has on the SW side a straight piece of wall about 20m long, once about 2m thick. and now 2m high towards the field, but on the other side almost level with the motte top. Tucked into a corner at the south end are traces of what may have been a small round tower. This castle has no known history but it is thought to have been built either by Bernard fitz Unspac, or by the Waldeboefs, who inherited lands here during Henry I's reign. Just 300m further north are traces of what looks like a 20m diameter ringwork, possibly a siege work erected by Llywelyn ab Iorwerth in the period 1217-34.

ALEXANDERSTONE MOTTES   SO 073301 & 070295

The farm cuts into the SE side of a motte 5m high and 10m by 15m on top, which has traces of a bailey 30m by 15m to the north. Beside a stream 1.5km to the south is a second mound 1m high with a summit 9m across and a ditch now mostly silted up. An Alexander mentioned in a charter concerned with Brecon Priory c1148 was probably a member of the Mora family, then lords here.

The hall block at Brecon

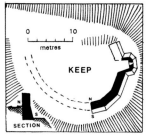

Brecon: plan of keep

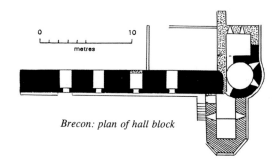

Brecon: plan of hall block

BRECON CASTLE   SO 043288   V

In 1093 Bernard Newmarch built a castle on the promontory above the confluence of the Usk and Honddu rivers. He was blockaded there by the Welsh in 1094 until relieved by Roger de Newburgh. A rampart and ditch defended a spade-shaped bailey 120m by 90m from the high ground to the north, where the original Norman town lay, and a large mound was raised in the NE corner overlooking the Honddu. Bernard's grandson Roger, Earl of Hereford, died without issue in 1155. The lordship (but not the earldom of Hereford) then passed in turn to three younger brothers, the last of whom, Mahel, perished when Bronllys Castle caught fire in 1165. Brecon then went to his sister Bertha, wife of Philip de Braose. Under him the settlement east of the Honddu was probably laid out and either he or his son William erected a polygonal shell keep on the motte. William fell out with King John in 1207 and lost the castle but it was recaptured by his brothers Giles and Reginald in 1215.

Llywelyn ap Iorweth attacked Brecon in 1217, 1231 and 1233, the new town being destroyed on the last of these occasions. Stone walls around the bailey were probably begun immediately afterwards and continued by Humphrey de Bohun, heir of the Earl of Hereford, who married the heiress Eleanor de Braose in 1241. The castle was entrusted to the keeping of Roger Mortimer in 1263 but was "shamefully surrendered" to Llwelyn ap Gruffydd after Roger was wounded in battle during the summer. Prince Edward captured Brecon shortly after his escape from Simon de Montfort's forces in 1265 but it was soon reoccupied by Llywelyn ap Gruffydd. Roger Mortimer was defeated by the Welsh Prince just outside the town during an attempt to recapture it in 1266. Brecon changed hands several times in 1273 before Humphrey VII de Bohun managed to obtain secure possession. The Welsh probably made another attempt to take the castle in 1295. Edward II took over the castle in 1322 after Humphrey VIII de Bohun, who erected the hall block c1300, was killed fighting against him in support of Thomas, Earl of Lancaster at Boroughbridge.

Henry, Duke of Lancaster, married Mary, heiress of Humphrey X de Bohun, who died in 1372. Duke Henry took the throne as Henry IV in 1399. Sir Thomas Berkeley held Brecon Castle for him against Owain Glyndwr, considerable repairs having been carried out on it in 1400-02. In 1404 Lord Berkeley and the Earl of Warwick were sent with 100 men-at-arms and 11 mounted archers to secure the castle. Brecon later passed to the Stafford Dukes of Buckingham, and the name Ely Tower given to the keep refers to Morton, Bishop of Ely, a captive within it during Richard III's reign (1483-5). The castle hall was given a magnificent new roof c1540 but it was dismantled in the early 17th century. Charles I was at Brecon in August 1645 but soon afterwards Colonel Turberville surrendered the castle after a short siege by Major General Laugharne. The defences were probably then slighted.

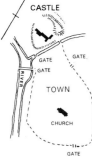

Brecon: site plan

Brecon Castle

The 15m high mound lies within the grounds of a house and its slopes have been terraced and planted. On the summit there survive three short sides of a multi-sided shell keep with a wall 1.7m thick above a battered plinth around an ovoid court 15m wide. Footings of a fourth side lie beyond a polygonal NE turret of later date containing a vaulted chamber with one tiny loop. South of the mound is the south wall of a hall block of c1300 with two levels of fine apartments above low cellars. Only the cusped single light upper windows are unrestored. The wall is 21m long and 2.4m thick above a plinth and ends on the east in a round turret against which abuts a later semi-polygonal latrine turret. Both turrets have traces of arrowloops, but have been much altered. The Buck brothers' engraving shows defensive walls further south, perhaps of a lower bailey, but these do not appear on Meredith Jones' plan of 1744. He shows the castle as having a gatehouse facing NW and a round tower keep with the shell wall as at Tretower. A building west of the hall was rebuilt to form a hotel by the Morgans of Tredegar Park, who purchased the site in 1809. The battlements on the hall wall also date from their time.

Jones also shows the layout of the now destroyed 13th century town walls which were flanked by ten towers (most of them probably round) and had four gates which were dismantled in 1785. Two gates lay close together facing the bridges over the Usk and Honddu, the Struet Gate giving access up to the priory lay on the north side and the Watton Gate lay at the SE end of the town. The line of the walls, which were repaired in 1404 during the Glyndwr revolt, is still fairly clear on the ground. A high rampart survives on the east and traces of a rectangular tower south of it.

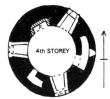

The keep at Bronllys

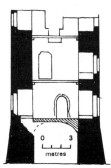

Bronllys: plans & section

BRONLLYS CASTLE   SO 149346   C

Although Richard Fitz Pons is said to have established a castle here in the 1090s, creating a motte out of a rock outcrop above the Afon Llynfi with an inner bailey of triangular shape extending 60m northwards and a wider outer bailey beyond, there is a possibility that the castle was founded by Walter Clifford to serve as the seat of Cantref Selyf, granted to him by Roger, Earl of Hereford in return for the service of five knights at the castle of Brecon. Paul Remfry has suggested that the original llys of the cantref lay at Llyswen, where there is a possible motte (the tree-clad stoney mound at SO 131376) close to an older fort. Giraldus Cambrensis mentions a stone falling from a tower in a fire in 1165 and killing the then lord of Brecon, Mahel. This suggests a stone building then existed here (unless the building was of wood but had stones high up it to secure the roof or as missiles to hurl down on attackers).

The existing round tower keep on the motte and the now-vanished inner bailey curtain wall are thought to have been built by Walter de Clifford II c1230. Although Cantref Selyf was attacked by Prince Dafydd in 1241 and 1244 Bronllys does not appear to have fallen. The castle was later held by the Mortimers and was taken from them by Edward II in 1322. The castle later passed to Humphrey Bohun of Brecon, then to Duke of Lancaster, becoming a Crown possession when Duke Henry took the throne in 1399. In 1444 Henry VI granted the stewardship of the castle to Nicholas Poyntz, and it was later held by Sir Roger Vaughan. The castle was given to Humphrey Stafford, 3rd Duke of Buckingham in 1508 and was said to be abandoned and ruined in 1521 when his estates were surveyed after his execution by Henry VIII. Bronllys was then given by the king to Sir David Williams but before long Sir Roger Vaughan of Porthaml had obtained the estate, which was later held in turn by the families of Knollys, Cecil, Morgan, Williams, Lewis and Davies. Part of the hall in the bailey, which is shown as a lofty building with fragments of a corbelled parapet on the Buck brothers' engraving, was incorporated into the stable-block of a new house built in the bailey in the 1790s.

The ruined keep is now maintained by Cadw and is reached direct from the Talgarth road, without any access through the bailey. It measures 9.8m in diameter above a high battered plinth capped by a roll-moulding and is over 16m high. The entrance doorway lies 4m above the base and was enclosed by a forebuilding. It has a drawbar hole to secure the door and leads into a hall 5.2m in diameter with two window embrasures, both with seats. One has a stair leading down towards the cellar below, which was provided with a dome-vault in a mid 14th century remodelling, when all the floor levels were raised up, and the topmost storey then added in place of the original battlements. The last 3m of the drop to the cellar floor had to be reached by a ladder. A stair curves round from the side of the other embrasure up to the private chamber above. This room has a fireplace and two ogee-headed windows, all 14th century alterations. Another stair leads up to the more ruined topmost storey, which was a bedroom with a fireplace, a latrine and three even spaced window embrasures with seats. The stair arrangements in this tower, with the necessity to cross each floor to get to the stair to the next, can hardly have been convenient in terms of privacy. No stairs lead up from this added topmost room, so the remodelled tower probably had a conical roof covering the walls as well, without a parapet.

Bronllys Castle as it was in 1741

BUILTH CASTLE   SO 044510   F

Impressive earthworks rise high above the Wye east of the town of Builth Wells. A motte rises 9m above a ditch 2m deep to a summit 17m across. A 90m long and 30m wide crescent-shaped bailey lies to the east and south and a smaller outer bailey to the west. A deep ditch with a high counterscarp bank surrounds the whole of the circular area. The counterscarp has been breached to allow water in this ditch to drain away. The original castle of the lordship of Buellt lay at Caer Beris. The first mention of a castle on the existing site is when it was fortified by the sheriff of Gloucester in 1208, but since the earthworks include a motte they may go back to at least the 1170s, unless the castle captured by the Welsh in 1168 lay here instead of at Caer Beris. The sheriff was soon forced to retire, but he returned to complete the work in 1210.

Giles and Reginald de Braose recaptured the castle from King John in 1215 and began to refortify it. After John died they made their peace with the regents acting for the young Henry III, who aided the construction of further defensive works at Builth by Reginald in 1219. Llywelyn ab lorwerth failed to capture the castle by siege in 1223, but it was surrendered to him in 1229 after he had captured William de Braose. After Llywelyn executed William in 1230 for having an affair with his wife during his captivity, Builth passed to Maud de Braose, who was married to one of the Mortimers, but the castle was only retaken from the Welsh in 1241 and then rebuilt in stone on the orders of Henry III under the supervision of John of Monmouth. Llywelyn ap Gruffydd failed in an attempt to storm the castle in 1260, but it was betrayed to him shortly afterwards and then destroyed.

Edward I had the castle rebuilt between 1277 and 1282 probably under the supervision of James of St George, who designed several of the royal castles along the North Wales coast. Over £1,666 was spent on the works, which were guarded by a garrison of about fifty men. There appears to have been a large round tower keep on the motte, possibly built on the base of a similar structure built in the 1240s, and it was probably surrounded by a low chemise wall. The inner bailey had a curtain wall flanked by six D-shaped towers and a twin-towered gatehouse, but only excavation could determine how much of this was a rebuilding of what what built in the 1240s. A force of nine horsemen and forty foot soldiers formed the garrison in 1277, although it was reduced the next year. In 1282 Llywelyn ap Gruffydd was killed in a skirmish nearby after unsuccessfully trying to persuade the garrison to surrender the castle to him. The prince's death removed the immediate threat to central Wales and the works at Builth soon came to a halt, the gatehouse of the inner bailey apparently not being completed as intended.

During the Welsh revolt of 1294 Builth was held by John Giffard and manned by three heavily armed horsemen, three lightly armed horsemen, twenty crossbowmen, and forty longbowmen. The de Bohuns held the castle in 1317 and they claimed custody of it in Edward III's reign, although it was actually held by various families for short periods, having been confiscated by Edward II after the Earl of Hereford was killed in a battle at Boroughbridge. During the Glyndwr rebellion of the early 15th century the castle was commanded by Lord Richard Grey of Codnor. The castle was probably abandoned in the latter part of the 15th century and most of the stonework later removed for the construction of buildings in the town.

CAERAU MOTTE   SN 923501   V

A farm lies in the SW end of a Roman fort platform. Set midway along the SW end of the fort is a 5m high motte.

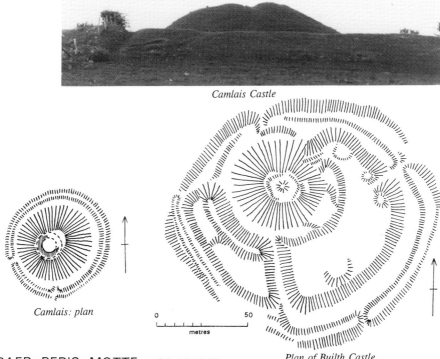

Camlais Castle

Camlais: plan

0   50

metres

Plan of Builth Castle

CAER BERIS MOTTE   SO 030507

Guarding the neck of a loop of the River Irfon just 1km west of Builth Wells is a mound rising 6m to a summit 22m long by 18m wide with traces of what likes like a former shell keep. A house of 1896-1911 lies within the site of the bailey. It is likely that the site was fortified by Philip Braose in the 1090s and was the seat of his lordship of Buellt. It may have been abandoned after capture and destruction by Rhys ap Gruffydd in 1168.

CAMLAIS CASTLE   SN 956261   V

This site is alternatively known as the castle of Blaencamlais, Cwm Camlais, Maescar or Dyfynoch. It looks from a distance like a large motte near the edge of flat moorland north of Brecon Beacons, but the top of the mound is actually the lower half of a circular tower 13m in diameter over walling 3m thick, mostly buried in its own debris. A doorway low down on the east side revealed by excavation in the 1980s is no longer visible. The tower is probably of mid 13th century date and has a surrounding ditch and counterscarp but no signs of any bailey or outbuildings. This tower was probably the new castle beyond Brecon captured by Prince Edward after his escape from incarceration by the adherents of Simon de Montfort in 1265. It could have been built either by Humphrey VI de Bohun to act as a forester's lodge and outpost beyond his main seat at Brecon, or it may have been built by Llewelyn ap Gruffydd. A 14th century document suggests that land in this district was given by Earl Humphrey VII to Einion Sais (probably after the earl regained this district in 1276) with the intention that the castle of Camlais would be strenthened.

Camlais Castle

CASTELL BLAENLLYNFI   SO 145229

After William Braose lost his estates to King John in 1208 a third of the county of Brecknock was given to Peter Fitz Herbert. He is assumed to have erected this castle as the seat of this new baronry between then and 1215, when Reginald de Braose seems to have forcibly taken possession of this district. The new castle would have superseded the more remotely sited fortress high up on a wind-swept hill at Castell Dinas. Blaenllynfi was returned to the Fitz Herberts two years later. It was captured and plundered by Llywelyn ab Iorwerth and Richard Marshal in October 1233, and it was captured in 1262 by Llywelyn ap Gruffydd. Reginald Fitz Peter Fitz Herbert recaptured the castle in 1273. It seems to have been in Mortimer hands when it was seized by Edward II after the failure of the rebellion of 1322, and it was then held by the Dispensers until their downfall in 1326. An inquistion of 1337 describes the castle and its numerous structural defects in some detail. It appears that most of the buildings had then been ruinous or at least seriously decayed for over half a century, and there is no evidence that any serious repairs were actually executed..

Castell Blaenllynfi

Castell Blaenllynfi

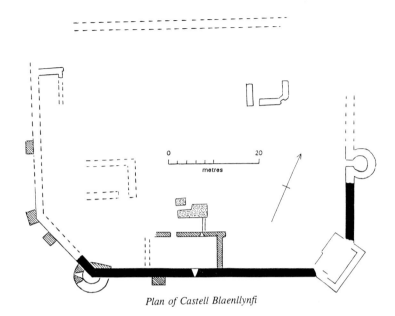

Plan of Castell Blaenllynfi

The remains lie hidden in woodland and are surrounded by a ditch which probably contained water held in by a dam at the NE corner. The main court 67m long from east to west by 50m wide was surrounded by a curtain wall 1.8m thick constructed of shale laid in a poor mortar. The base of the south side remains, plus a section on the east which stands complete to the wall-walk, althigh its boldly projecting plinth has been defaced. The entrance seems to have been at the NE corner, where the evidence of the layout is rather confused, but a rectangular building of some size lay immediately west of it. Only the slightest traces remain of a boldly projecting rectangular building about 17m by 8m at the NW corner. This may have been "Le holestour" a five storey tower that the 1337 survey reported as needing its joists and roof renewed at a cost of £10. Little remains of the curtain wall between here and the chamfered off SW corner, but more survives of the buttresses later added to strengthen it. A round tower 7.2m in diameter retaining two arrow-slits (probably the Nurse's Tower of the survey) was later added here, perhaps in the 1250s. Against the south side are remains of a building 16m by 7m, probably the hall which needed rebuilding in 1327 at an estimated cost of £100. East of it is a well, whilst a chamber block lay west of it. At the SE corner is the base of a rectangular tower 10m by 8m set diagonally, probably the "Turbeville Tower" described in the survey as needing £100 worth of repairs. If this is correct the D-shaped tower which projected from the east curtain wall (probably another addition of the 1250s) must have been the Picard Tower, a four storeytstructure, the roof of which collapsed in the late 13th century. The survey also mentions the single storey "Knight's Chamber" which had a latrine and needed total rebuilding, as did the kitchen, larder, granary, bakehouse, brewery and grange, which had recently collapsed, a chapel with a wine cellar underneath, and a water supply piped in from outside the walls. Ovens on the north side may show where the kitchen and bakehouse lay. There was also a low outer wall on the east and south sides of the castle but few traces of it remain.

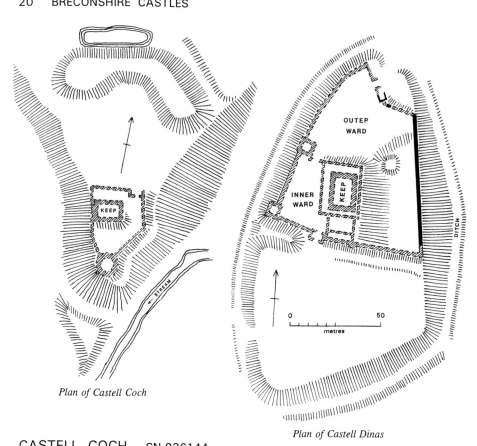

Plan of Castell Coch

Plan of Castell Dinas

CASTELL COCH   SN 936144

This castle took its name from the red sandstone of which it was constructed. It lies on a promontory about 9m high between the Afon Llia and Afon Dringarth in a remote position on the south side of the Brecon Beacons. The only reference to it is in 1239, when it was held by William de Braose. The castle may have served as a mustering point for the Marcher lords in the war of 1276-7, and in this vicinity the rebel Llewelyn Bren surrendered to the Bohuns in 1316. The southern end of the promontory bears the overgrown lower part of a wall about 1.5m thick around a pentangular court 27m wide. Adjoining the west wall and occupying much of the rectangular northern half of the court is a hall keep about 18m long by 12m wide over walling 2m thick, which probably contained just a single room over a dark basement. At the NE corner are signs of a recessed gateway. The southern part of the court tapers to an acute angle which was occupied by a round tower about 13m in external diameter, large enough to be regarded as a second keep. The layout and the poor quality of the curtain and round tower masonry suggest they could have been added in 1260s by Llywelyn ap Gruffydd to a keep built a couple of generations earlier. If so then the round tower would have also only contained a living room over a dark basement since other Welsh towers of this period rarely had more than two storeys. North of the court is a bailey 60m wide protected on the vulnerable north side by a high and wide rampart with a ditch in front of it, half of which is water filled.

Castell Dinas

CASTELL DINAS   SO 179301

Castell Dinas may be the "Waynard's Castle" mentioned in 1143-55 and was the original seat of the lordship of Blaenllynfi granted by King John to Peter Fitz Herbert in 1208 after the de Broaose family were forfeited. Reginald de Braose took back much of his father's lands in 1215 and Fitzherbert only obtained a secure title to the lordship by marrying an heiresses of William de Braose after the latter's execution by Llywelyn. In 1233 Dinas was one of the castles captured by Richard Marshal, Earl of Pembroke, when he rebelled against Henry III. All of Fitzherbert's sons died in the 1240s and Henry III granted Dinas along with the more recent castle at Blaenllynfi to Walerand de Teys. Subsequently, under the Mortimers, Blaenllynfi formed the seat of the lordship. However, Dinas seems to have remained garrisoned until at least 1326. It is assumed to have been captured by Llewelyn ap Gruffydd in 1263 and to have been retaken by the English a few years later. Early in 1322 the castle was surrendered by the Mortimers, but they regained it in 1326, after which it was probably abandoned. Leyland's description of c1540 suggests it was then as ruinous as it is now, and he reports the castle as having been destroyed by the local inhabitants (presumably in support of Owain Glyndwr) during the reign of Henry IV.

The castle lies at 450m on an isolated foothill of the Black Mountains qand is the highest castle site in Britain. Although little remains apart from buried footings and much fallen debris, the site is of interest as being a castle of some size with walls, towers and a keep all likely to predate the early 13th century. The keep and possibly the inner ward may even predate the construction of the castle at Brecon in 1093. A ditch cuts an eye-shaped Iron Age hillfort 180m long by 83m wide into two, the whole site being surrounded by a deep ditch and a counterscarp. The northern part was surrounded by a wall up to 2m thick which still remains in a very ruinous state as part of a modern boundary on the lower east side. At the north end was a re-entrant angle with a postern gateway flanked by a small tower on the south side and protected externally by a barbican. The tower is the only other part of the ruins where walling not obscured by debris stands above the footings. It has a damaged pointed-arched opening facing towards the court. The highest part of the bailey is the SW corner which is filled by an inner ward which is roughly a square of 38m and has footings of a gatehouse on the south and square towers at the SW and NW corners. East of the latter was a second gateway. The west wall remains suggest a thickness of about 2.5. The internal height to the wall-walk may only have been about 3m but the external height would have been much greater. The eastern half of the inner ward is occupied by the remains of a rectangular keep about 22m long by 14m wide within a chemise wall probably taking the form of a platform with high retaining walls upon which were parapets around the base of the keep. Between the chemise and the inner ward wall east of the south gate there seems to have been a building, a space being left between it and the curtain to permit south facing windows.

Remains of keep at Castell Dinas

CASTELL DU   SN 917284

Of a 13th century castle alternately known as Castell Rhyd-Y-Briw only fragments remain of the south wall of the court together with a the 6m high outer part of a U-shaped tower 8m in diameter. A bungalow encroaches on the northern part of the bailey platform, which lies above the confluence of the Usk and Senni just west of Sennybridge. This may have been the castle begun by Llywelyn ap Gruffydd in 1262. In 1271 Castell Du was occupied by Llywellyn's ally Einion Sais, who is traditionally said to have had a second castle at Penpont, where a tributary stream flows into the River Usk halfway between Castell Du and Brecon, although his other seat may have actually been the tower at Cwm Camlais 4km SE of Castell Du. A pair of World War II pill-boxes lie at either ends of the curtain wall, modern recognition of the strategic importance of the site. Both pillboxes may stand on the bases of former towers.

Castell Du

Plan of Castell Du

CASTELL MADOC   SO 125370

The Powell family are said to have had their seat here since the 1090s.
From that time may date the 6m high motte with a 3m high counterscarp on the east.
The summit measures 22m east-west by 18m north-south. The bailey south of the
motte is said to have been given a curtain wall in the 14th century but there are no
obvious remains of such. The bailey site is now occupied by a house bearing a
datestone of 1588 with the initials of Thomas Powell. This was remodelled in the late
17th century and has 19th century additions.

On higher ground just 75m NE of the motte is a square ringwork 25m across with
round corners. Excavations in the 1960s showed that the rampart had been 1.5m
high and 5m wide, the material having come from a ditch of similar dimensions. As
there was little evidence of extended occupation the site was assunmed to be a
siegework, possibly of 1168, but more likely of the 1230s.

CILWHYBERT MOTTE   SO 014268

By a farm on the south side of Afon Tarell is a fine motte rising 7m from a ditch 2m
deep which was water-filled except on the south side in the early 20th century, when
the mound was overgrown. The mound summit is 13m in diameter. The very worn
down ringwork about 35m in diameter on the north bank of the river beside Pont
Estyll 0.5km to the west (at SO 009270) may be a siegework raised against the
castle at Cilwybert by Llewelyn ap Iorwerth c1217-34.

CLAWYD BRITISH RINGWORK   SO 862369

A ringwork measuring 42m by 30m with a rampart 2.5m high above the ditch lies in
an isolated position 340m above sea level on the Sennybridge Artillery Range.

CRICKADARN RINGWORKS   SO 088421 & 059413   V

Not far west of the church is a D-shaped ringwork 50m across with a ditch 3 or 4m
deep all round except towards the main ridge where it appears to have been filled in.
The straight north side overlooks a slope. The NW corner has traces od a possible
round tower. The other sides had a counterscarp bank and also some protection from
marshland. Another D-shaped ringwork lies above a slope 2km to the west at 360m.
It has a rampart and ditch which are pierced for an entrance on the SE side.

Cilwybert Motte

Crickhowell Castle

Barbican remains, Crickhowell

CRICKHOWELL CASTLE   SO 218183   F

In the 12th century the Turbevilles probably supplemented Maes Celyn motte with a large new motte and bailey castle on this flat platform slightly above the Usk. Rebuilding in stone began under Sir Grimbald Pauncefoot of Gloucestershire, who married the heiress Sybil Turbeville c1264. The work was continued after his death in 1287 by his sons Grimbald, who died in 1315, and Emeric, who was dispossessed by Edward II in 1322 for his support of the Mortimers. The castle has an alternative name of Alisby's Castle from the name of another of the knights serving Roger Mortimer. Emeric's son Sir Grimbald recovered the castle and his brother Hugh's son John held it against Owain Glyndwr in 1403. When the Pauncefoot line ended in the mid 15th century the castle was claimed by Richard, Duke of York, who married a Mortimer heiress. His son Edward IV granted Crickhowell to his supporter Sir William Herbert. By that time the castle may have been in decay and the buildings were subsequently robbed of their stone for erecting other buildings in the town.

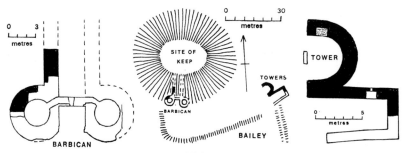

Plans of Crickhowell Castle

The 15m high mound bears the last traces of a shell keep enclosing a court about 24m long by 15m wide. It probably had several D-shaped flanking towers and was reached by steps from the NW corner of a bailey about 55m square. The foot of the steps was guarded by a barbican with round towers 6m in diameter flanking a drawbridge pit. The bases of the towers remain and the NW quadrant of the western tower survives to full height, showing evidence of a basement, two upper storeys with fireplaces, and battlements. Old drawings show that the vanished bailey wall had a square tower at the SE corner and a round tower at the SW corner. The NE corner still has a D-shaped tower 8m wide still standing three storeys high complete with battlements, although the latter may be a modern reconstruction. This tower possibly originally formed part of a gatehouse. Adjoining it on the south is a rectangular tower of slightly later date which was at least 10m long by 5.6m wide externally. Only the north wall now survives above the level of the lowest of four storeys. The bailey walls must have been substantially complete by 1281 when the townsfolk obtained a murage grant for the construction of a town wall which has now survived. With Prince Llywelyn being killed only two years later and the Welsh threat consequently receding, the work on the town walls may not have been completed, if indeed it was ever begun. The folly tower of much later date standing in Tower Street has no connection with either the castle or town defences. A drawing of 1805 by Hoare shows the castle much as it is now except that he appears to show a broad wet moat east of the castle bailey.

FFOREST TWDIN   SN 919520

A tiny rectangular court 8m by 4m is enclosed by a rampart and a water-filled rock-cut ditch on the three sides away from the steep drop on the NW side.

GARN COCH MOTTE   SO 213477

The small motte on a flat, low lying site is almost worn away.

GARN-Y-CASTELL   SO 158297   V

The very worn down ringwork 1.5m high and 30m across on a spur 2km west of Castell Dinas may have been erected by Humphrey Visdelou in the late 11th century. By 1144 the lands here had reverted to the Earls of Hereford and had been granted to Brecon Priory, the castle having presumably been dismantled.

Interior of keep at Hay Castle

HAY CASTLE   SO 229423   O

The "castello de haia" is mentioned in 1121 and the keep could go back to that period. Matilda St Valery, wife of William de Braose, is said to have built the stone keep c1200 but it is more likely she added the curtain wall to an already existing tower standing on the north side of a large ringwork. She died of starvation whilst incarcerated in Windsor Castle at the command of King John, who seized the castle at Hay in 1208. Giles and Reginald de Braose captured the castle in 1215, but abandoned it in 1216 at King John swept through the Marches. The castle and town were then burnt, and the town suffered a similar fate at the hands of Llewellyn ab lorwerth in 1231. The castle constable, Walter Godarville, was tricked by the monks of Cwmhir into an ambush beside the river, but the castle may have held out since in 1233 it was used by Henry III as a base for his campaign against Walter Clifford. In 1232 and 1237 the king granted the townsfolk of Hay the right to collect a special toll to pay for walling the town in stone. Hay later passed to the de Bohuns.

In 1263 Henry III took the castle from Humphrey de Bohun VI and gave it to Roger Mortimer. His commander, Walter Hackelutel surrendered the castle to the forces commanded by Simon de Mortfort in 1264, but Roger Mortimer recaptured Hay in 1265. From here he mounted his uncessessful attempt to retake Brecon in 1266. Hay was eventually returned to the Bohuns and used by them as a base for the recapture of their main seat at Brecon in 1273. It was seized by Edward II after the failure of the rebellion of 1322, which the de Bohuns supported. The castle was said to be worth £50 in 1362, and seems to have been kept in repair during the 14th century.

Both town and castle suffered damage by Owain Glyndwr's forces in 1400 but the castle was listed as defensible against the Welsh rebels in 1403. By then Hay had passed to the Earls of Stafford, who later became Dukes of Buckingham. The castle is said to have been damaged during the conflicts of the 1460s. Edward Stafford, 3rd Duke of Buckingham, remodelled the keep. He was executed by Henry VIII on trumped up charges of treason in 1521. Whatever apartments then adjoined the keep were swept away in the 1660s when James Boyle of Hereford built a new mansion. Most of the curtain wall was demolished either to improve views from the mansion or to defortify the site during the Civil War. In the early 19th century the house was occupied by the Wellington family, who purchased it from Glyn family heiresses. The house was restored c1910 but the eastern part was gutted by fire in 1939. The western part was in turn gutted by fire in 1979 but was restored and is now used for second-hand book selling, for which the town of Hay is now famous.

Hay Castle from the south

The town walls enclosed a D-shaped area with the straight side facing the River Wye. The castle lay on the south side with the West gate nearby. To the east was the Black Lion Gate and to the north the Water Gate, all removed in the late 18th century. The last section of the wall on the west was removed in the 1860s to make way for the railway (now long closed).

The keep measures 10m from north to south by 8.3m wide, making it one of the smallest in Britain. It guards the existing gateway (the present vehicular access to the castle from the west is 20th century) and it is possible that prior to the first of several rebuilds necessitated by poor foundations, the gateway was through the lowest level of the keep, two thirds of which is now full of rubble. The second storey room has the remains of a Late Norman window of two lights facing the court and above it is a better preserved specimen, lacking only the mullion between the two round-arched lights set under a round outer arch. No other original features now survive and there is no stair, there being little room for one within the thin walls. The only means of access to the third storey, which has a small chamber in the NE corner, was by a doorway, now blocked from the later mansion on the west side. At some time the northern corners were provided with heavy buttressing and c1500 the sends and third storey rooms were given fireplaces in a rebuilt north wall with two-light windows flanking each one. The fireplaces and window embrasures both have wooden lintels. In an earlier rebuilding, perhaps after damage caused by the Welsh in 1231, the whole SE corner was replaced and buttressed and a new doorway made alongside it facing east. At the same time the outer arch of the gateway was added, providing the slot for a portcullis worked from a small chamber at the height of the curtain wall-walk 7m above the court. The wall-walk, portcullis room and keep doorway are reached by a stair beside the keep SE corner which turns to rise over the back of the gateway. The 12m long section of curtain east of the gateway is all that remains of the wall around the courtyard, which was about 75m from east to west by 65m wide. The wall is 1.8m thick at the top but is 3m thick at the base, having a high plinth of complex section suggesting a late 12th century date.

The 3m high mound with a summit 20m across near the parish church seems to have formed the seat of the manor of Melinog held independently of the main castle so the two sites may have both been occupied simultaniously rather than the stone castle having superseded this site. It may have been built by William Revel, one of Bernard de Newmarch's knights and possibly had a bailey to the NE.

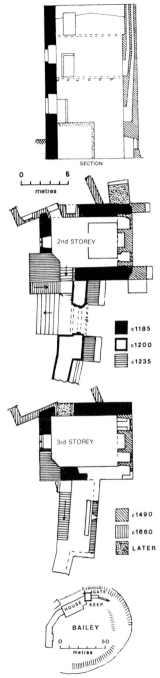

Hay: plans & section

HEN CASTELL   SO 213166   V

This may have formed a seat of the Turbevilles prior to the construction of stone buildings at Crickhowell 2km to the north. Sited where natural spings abound, it consisted of a wet-moated platform 23m square and 2m high with the southern part filled by the footings of a rectangular keep 23m long by 15m wide over walls 2.5m thick.

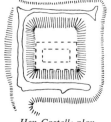

Hen Castell: plan

LLANFAN MOTTE   SN 967566

SW of the church is a ringwork with a ditch and counterscarp bank.

LLANDDEW PALACE   SO 055308   V

In the grounds of the vicarage north of Llanddew church are remains of a palace of the bishops of St Davids. Two fragments remain of a two storey hall block on the north side which may be a relic of the house Giraldus Cambrensis had here in the 1170s, although Leland refers to the archdeacons of Brecon (Gerald was archdeacon and never attained his goal of obtaining the bishopric) as having a separate house, both dwellings being ruinous in his day. It is just possible that the semi-fortfied enclosure roughly 100m square was contained both dwellings. It was probably here in 1291 that the earls of Gloucester and Hereford were tried on the orders of Edward I for conducting a private war over possession of the northern part of Senghennydd. The hall block was 20m long by 10.5m wide over walls 1.2m thick and contains one small lower window traces of two bigger ones higher up. On the west side is part of a curtain wall with a well set under a chamfered arch. This well is attributed to Bishop Gower (i.e. c1340), but the wall (now lacking most of its mortar) is more likely to be 13th century. Part of a small round solid turret remained north of the well until the mid 20th century. The wall on the south side seems modern, although a doorway probably of 14th century date has been reset in it.

Llanddew Palace

Well at Llanddew

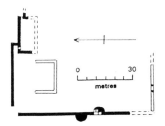

Plan of Llanddew Palace

Archway at Llanddew

LLANDEFAELOG FACH MOTTE   SO 033323

West of the church is a tree-clad motte rising 3m above the ground to the south where a house of 1630 stands on the site of the bailey, and much more above the stream to the south. The summit measures 15m across.

LLANTHOMAS MOTTE   SO 209403

A worn down motte damaged on the west side lies beside the Digedi Brook. There are signs of a surrounding ditch. The bailey may have laid to the south, since when a bungalow was built on the platform to the west and north in the 1980s no sign of an enclosure there was revealed.

LLYSDINAM MOTTE   SN 998584

A ringwork 13m across lies on a spur high above the Estyn Brook. The 2m high rampart and the ditch are discontinued on the south, where there is a cliff.

MAES CELYN MOTTE   SO 095248

This tree-clad mound with the last traces of a stone tower about 9m square on the southern part of the two level summit was an outwork or predecessor of the more low-lying Crickhowell Castle 1.5km to the SE, and thus was an early seat of the Turbeville family. The motte stands about 3m above a bailey platform to the SE.

PENCELLI CASTLE   SO 095248

Pencelli Castle was probably built by Ralph Baskerville, one of Bernard de Newmarch's knights, in the 1090s. It was the seat of an important lordship originally owing four and a half knights fees towards the defence of the castle at Brecon. After Robert Baskerville died c1210 Pencelli passed via his daughter to the Le Wafre family. The castle was captured by Giles and Reginald de Braose in 1215 and by Richard Marshal in 1233. Reginald later settled the castle upon his wife Gwladys Ddu, the daughter of Llywelyn ab Iorwerth in return for the territories of Kerry and Cedewain. She later married Ralph Mortimer who thus claimed Pencelli. The dispute was only finally settled when one of William de Braose's daughters married Ralph's son Roger, who seems to have built a new gatehouse and curtain wall at Pencelli in the 1270s. The castle was confiscated by Edward II in 1322 and given to Hugh Despenser the younger. It was later a Crown possession until Edward IV granted it to the Herberts. A new house was built in the late 16th century to replace the dilapidated domestic buildings. Richard Herbert sold Pencelli to his brother-in-law Captain Thomas Powell of Llanishen in the late 17th century.

The castle originally seems to have consisted of a ringwork at the projecting north corner, strongly defended by natural slopes, of a rectangular bailey 110m long by 90m wide. By the end of the 12th century the ringwork was superseded by a tower keep 14m square of which parts of the 3m thick NE and NW walls can still be seen in a clump of trees and shrubs, together with part of a second building. The Buck brothers engraving of 1741 shows two walls of the keep still standing three storeys high. In front of it they show a gatehouse with twin round towers and a fragment of a curtain wall with a pair of lancet windows. Nothing now remains of these but the house also shown is still inhabited. It bears the year 1583 on the main door and may be largely of that date. It is, however, much altered, and has reset medieval material including a late 15th century window with a segmental head, and parts of two late Norman windows (probably from the keep) with grooved heads, one of which has been set upside down. Inside are arches possible from the castle chapel.

PYTINDU MOTTE   SO 047310

Castle mounds once lay at both the farms of Pytindu and Pytingwyn.

Pencelli Castle as it was in 1741

SCETHROG TOWER   SO 105249

On flat ground beside the River Usk is a much altered 12th or 13th century tower built by a descendant of Milo Picard. There are a few traces of a moated enclosure to the west but no other medieval walls or outbuildings remain. The tower is now the home of the jazz musician George Melly. It measures about 11m square over walls 2m thick which are battered for much of their height. Above a low cellar which has long been inaccessible is a room set a few steps up from ground level. There is one more full storey above, plus attics in the gabled roof. In the later medieval period there may have been an attic within a wall-walk and parapet. The only original features now remaining are an altered upper storey fireplace, a pointed doorway to a now disused staircase which probably led up to the lost battlements, and parts of two lower storey window embrasures. The other features are of the 16th and 17th centuries and the dividing walls of the rooms are still later.

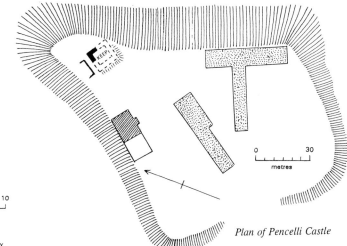

Plan of Pencelli Castle

1st STOREY

2nd STOREY

Scethrog Tower: plans

Scethrog Tower

Talgarth Tower

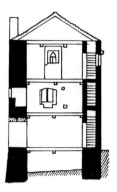

Talgarth Tower: plans

TALGARTH TOWER   SO 154337   V

On the east bank of the River Enig running through Talgarth village (and west of the church) is a much altered medieval tower of uncertain date. Probably it existed by 1282 when Reginald Fitz Peter Fitz Herbert was holding court twice a year in Talgarth. A castle here is mentioned in 1322, when it was confiscated by Edward II. Leland refers to the only notable buildings in the town as being the church and a prison standing near it. The 1741 Buck Brothers print shows a tower-like building standing NE of the church and indeed the farm 90m north of the church bears the name Tower Farm, so possibly there was a second tower there once. The surviving tower measures 8.2m by 7.8m and rises 9.5m to the eaves of a late 17th or early 18th century pyramidal roof which has probably replaced a parapet. The tower has a low cellar below ground level to the east and three upper storeys connected by straight staircases in the NE end wall. Modern buildings adjoin both end walls and have obscured the original entrance arrangements but the doorway is likely to have been in the NE wall one stage above ground level. The fireplaces are later replacements but original latrines and pointed windows with embrasures remain in the side walls. The latrine of the topmost storey was corbelled out like that on the early 13th century keep at Longtown in Herefordshire.

The motte at Trecastle

TRECASTLE MOTTE   SN 882292

This is the best preserved motte and bailey castle in Breconshire. An oval tree-clad motte 6m high occupies the east half of a bailey platform 115m long by 45m wide. Circumstantial evidence suggests the castle was built by Bernard de Newmarch c1095 and fell to a Welsh attack sometime between 1121 and 1136. It was probably then abandoned although possibly rebuilt in the 1150s by Walter Clifford.

TREDUSTAN MOTTE   SO 140324

A farmyard cuts into one side of a motte rising 4.5m to a summit 15m across.

TREFECA MOTTE   SO 145314 & 142323

A house now lies within the bailey which has strong natural slopes on each side except to the SE. The construction of the railway from Hay to Brecon caused removal of most of the motte in the NW corner, leaving just a chord of the summit which is 6m long, 2.5m high, and now overgrown. A predecessor or siege-camp ringwork 25m across lies on the hillside 1km to the SE.

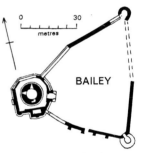

Tretower: site plan

Tretower Castle

TRETOWER CASTLE SO 185213 C

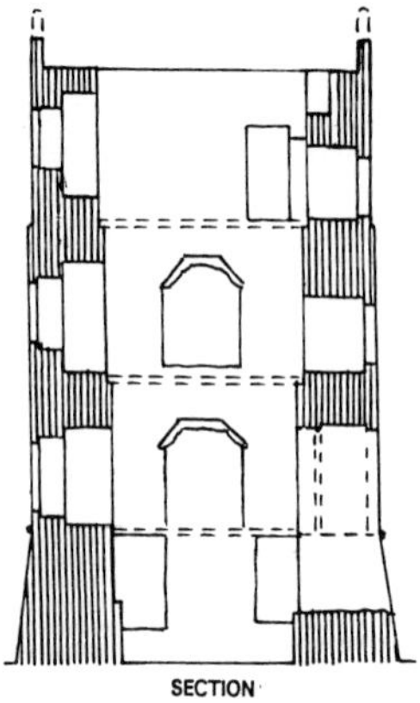
SECTION

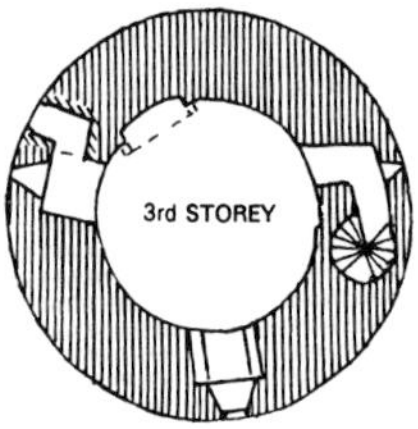
3rd STOREY

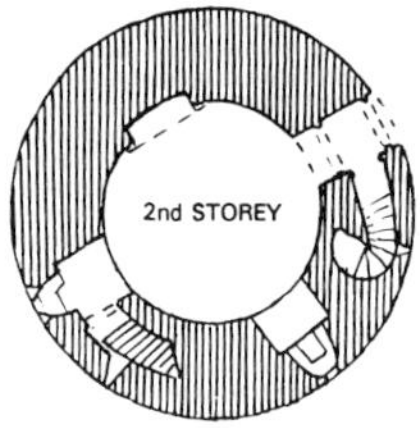
2nd STOREY

One of Bernard Newmarch's knights, built a modest stone revetted motte with a triangular bailey here c1100. Although low-lying the site was strongly defended by marshes and water-filled moats fed by the Rhiangoll Brook. His son or grandson Roger Picard acquired the additional lordship of Scethrog or Llansantffraed which enabled him c1160 to build at Tretower a stone shell keep with a hall, solar and kitchen inside it. After the castle was captured and destroyed by the Welsh in 1233 another Roger Picard enclosed the bailey with curtain walls with two round corner towers with high battered plinths and the domestic buildings within the shell keep were replaced by a round tower keep. The castle was held out against a Welsh attack in 1245 and the top storey of the keep may have been added afterwards to provide a more effective observation point commanding the valley. In 1262 another Roger Picard avoided a Welsh attack by allying himself with Llewelyn ap Gruffydd.

When John Picard died in 1308 the castle was said to be worth nothing because of its state of decay. The lordship passed to the Bluets of Ragland who developed Tretower Court just 80m to the SE, the east range there being early 14th century. The lords must have felt safe enough to live outside the walls after The Welsh defeat of 1282. However in 1403 the Bluets' descendant James Berkeley was ordered by Henry IV to refortify the decayed castle against Owain Glyndwr, and a Buck print of 1741 shows the shell keep as still then almost intact. In 1432 Lord Berkeley sold Tretower to his mother's second husband Sir William ap Thomas. The lordship and manor still belong to the Duke of Beaufort, a descendant of Sir William's son William Herbert. The latter, however, gave Tretower Court to his mother Gwladys' eldest son by her first marriage, Sir Roger Vaughan, who remodelled the house to serve as his residence.

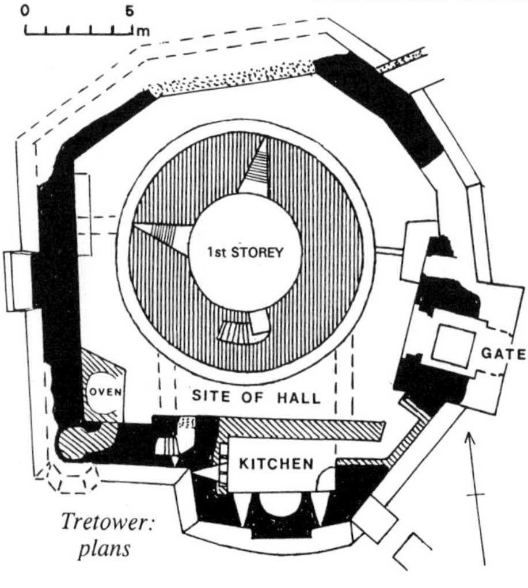
0
5
m
1st STOREY
GATE
OVEN
SITE OF HALL
KITCHEN

Tretower: plans

In c1480-5 Sir Roger's son Thomas added the gatehouse and curtain wall on the south side to create an impressive show front. However since the house was thinly walled with large windows on the other sides, and as far as is known had no moat, it would not have been defensible. Further alterations to Tretower Court were made by Charles Vaughan c1630. The direct male line died out with his grandson Edward and the Morgans who succeeded and took the name Vaughan eventually moved elsewhere, leasing the house to a farmer. It was handed over to the State after purchase by the Brecknock Society, both court and castle now being maintained by Cadw.

The shell wall is 1.8m thick above a battered plinth acting as a retaining wall to the small motte. It is broken down on the north and on the east, where there is the base of a small gatehouse 5m deep by 6m wide with a shallow pit below the passageway. The SW corner of the shell wall collapsed in 1947. It contained a spiral staircase connecting an office with a solar above, of which all that remains are a window and blocked fireplace in the shell wall. A second window served the hall to the east. South of the hall was a projection containing the kitchen, which still has an original fireplace flanked by two loops, but the inner wall is of later date.

The tower keep in the middle of the shell is 11m in diameter over walls 2.8m thick above a high battered plinth. The entrance passage gives onto a hall with a hooded fireplace and two window embrasures from one of which a stair curves down to a basement lighted only with two loops with the sills steeply stepped down. From the entrance passage is a spiral stair to the solar and upper levels. The solar also has a hooded fireplace and two windows. The doorway opening out of the side of one of the embrasures led to a block added later against the keep, probably during the Glyndwr revolt. The top storey is marked by an external offset which is continued across a staircase loop in the form of a transom. There is no fireplace.

The bailey is now mostly filled with farm buildings and is not accessible to the public. It has a fragmentary curtain wall 1.5m thick. There are foundations of a tower 7m in diameter at ground level at the south corner and buttresses set against the wall linking it to the shell. More stands of an east corner tower. The gatehouse probably lay midway between the two towers.

TYMAUR MOTTE

SO 125257

This is either a motte of sandstone slabs with a summit 15m by 12m, or the buried base of a round tower like Cwm Camlais.

Tretower: fireplace in keep

Tretower Castle

GAZETTEER OF CASTLES IN MONTGOMERYSHIRE

BISHOP'S MOAT   SO 291896   V

Elevated at 340m on the border with Shropshire is a motte rising 6m to a summit 13m across on the west side of an oval bailey 100m long by 65m wide. The castle is assumed to have been built by the Bishop of Hereford in the 1120s, possibly as a predecessor of their seat at Bishop's Castle, lower down not far to the east. This site may be the Castell Hithoet captured in 1233 by Llywelyn ap Iorwerth.

BRONFELIN MOTTE   SO 052913

This 4m high mound with a summit 10m across and a triangular bailey 27m wide by 48m long to the NE lie above a steep slope to the NW. They served as an outpost to the larger but more low lying major earthwork castle of Rhos Ddiarbed just 1km to the SW.

BRYN DERWEN MOTTE   SO 163852

The farm lies on the site of a bailey of a big quarried-away motte.

CAER SIAC MOTTE   SO 129972

The oval motte was much damaged when new tracks were made over and beside it in the 1960s, and two baileys have also been destroyed.

The motte at Bishop's Moat

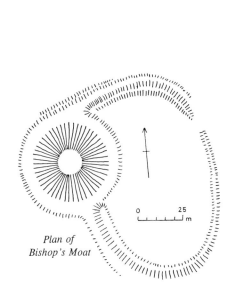

*Plan of
Bishop's Moat*

Dolforwyn Castle

CARREGHOFA CASTLE   SJ 255222 or 254218

The earthwork lying above a steep drop to the River Cynllaith may be the site of the castle built in 1101 by Robert de Bellesme and taken by Henry I's forces in 1102. It was repaired and garrisoned by Henry II in 1159-62 and was captured in 1163 by Owain Cyfeiliog and Owain Fychan. It was recovered by Henry II in 1165 but in 1187 the castle was occupied by Owain Fychan. He was killed during a night attack on the castle by his cousins Gwenwynwyn and Cadwallon. In 1194 the castle was recaptured for the English Crown and then given a stone curtain wall. It was then of some importance because of nearby silver mines. In 1197 the castle was handed over to Gwenwynwyn in order to secure the release of his prisoner Gruffydd ap Rhys, the ruler of Deheubarth. In 1212-13 Robert de Vipont rebuilt the castle for King John. It is assumed to have been destroyed by Llywelyn ap Iorwerth in the 1230s and to have not been restored. A rampart enclosed the 27m long side and 13m long east side of what is now a modest triangular court but which either before collapse of a cliff or quarrying was probably a rectangle three times as large. An alternative possible site for the stone castle is at Carreghofa Hall to the south where in 1871 a square room with plastered wall and other foundations of unknown date were found below the house and an adjacent field.

CASTLE CAEREINION   SJ 163054   F

The churchyard seems to have formed the bailey of a much worn-down motte in the north corner erected in 1156 by Madoc ap Maredudd. It passed to his nephew Owain Cyfeiliog, who went into exile after he took the side of the Normans soon after joining a Welsh alliance. With Norman support he later captured and destroyed the castle and killed all the garrison installed by his cousin Owain Fychan.

CASTELL MOCH   SJ 112246

The damaged motte by a farm probably had a summit diameter of about 23m.

CEFNBRYNTALCH MOTTE   SO 175963

A rocky hilltop 21m wide is divided into inner and outer enclosures 33m and 40m long respectively with an approach on the SW side.

Dolforwyn Castle

DOLFORWYN CASTLE   SO 153950

Llywelyn ap Gruffydd had this castle under construction in 1273 as a snub to the authority of Edward I, whose castle of Montgomery lay only 7km to the east..It was also to help keep the Prince of Powys in check. The work was probably well advanced by 1274 when Llywelyn stayed at the castle and whilst there discovered that the Prince of Powys (no doubt upset by the building of Dolforwyn) was party to a plot against him. The Prince of Powys was given custody of the castle after it was surrendered to Henry de Lacy and Roger Mortimer in April 1277 following Llywelyn's failure to relieve a siege against it. An inventory of 1322, when Edward II's forces seized the castle from Roger Mortimer, mentions a chapel, hall, lady's chamber, bakehouse, kitchen and brewery. The castle is unlikely to have been much used afterwards and is said to have been ruinous by the 1390s.

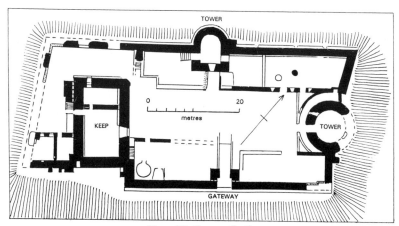

Plan of Dolforwyn Castle

The castle lies on a ridge above the west bank of the River Severn. Excavations by Cadw have revealed the lower parts of all the walls, of which only a few higher fragments were formerly visible above the accumulated earth and debris. A wall 1.6m thick above a broad battered base surrounds a court 65m by 27m. Set astride the line of the NE wall are remains of a tower 11m in diamter over walls 2.2m thick. The part of the tower facing the field is entirely destroyed. Near the middle of the long NW side is the base of a U-shaped tower 8m wide with its basement somewhat below courtyard level. The round tower is large enough to be considered a keep but there is also a keep-like rectangular building 19m long by 12.3m over walls 2.2m thick which mostly fills the SW third of the court, with its end wall forming part of the SE curtain wall, although set back from the line of the curtain further north. This building has a basement doorway on the SW side next to the foot of an external stair to the destroyed upper storey. The very large window facing NE towards the main court must surely be a later insertion to allow a former cellar to be used for a more domestic purpose, perhaps an office. It was perhaps then also that the NW end was divided off to make a strongroom, its doorway having a drawbar slot. In the south corner is a shute for a latrine serving the upper room. Two other shutes serving latrines in the uppermost rooms of the adjacent range lie nearby, and beside the east corner is a shute from a latrine on the curtain wall-walk, which was reached by an external stair beside this corner. There is another stair opposite serving the wall-walk on the NW side. The principal chambers of the castle lay between this second stair and the north corner. Beyond the U-shaped tower a set of rooms have been exposed with a large central pier and several windows and doorways facing the court. The pillar perhaps supported the fireplace of the hall above, with a chamber south of it and a bedroom in the U-shaped tower. East of this tower is a cistern deep down in the rock. The passages on either side of the round tower possibly contained stairs to the hall and to chambers over the service rooms along the SE side. The gateway in the middle of this side was unflanked but faced a steep slope and could only be reached by circumnavigating a considerable length of the castle wall by beams of a flat berm 2m wide. This gateway and the passage leading up into the court from it were later blocked and presumably replaced by a gateway at the unflanked SW end.

Dolforwyn Castle

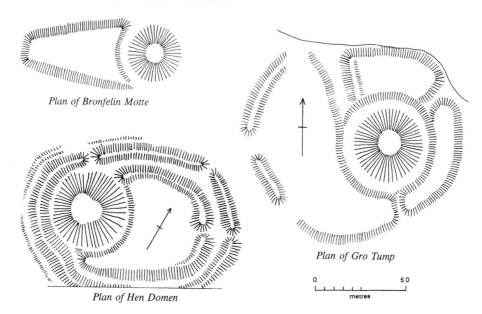

Plan of Bronfelin Motte

Plan of Gro Tump

Plan of Hen Domen

0   50

metres

GRO TUMP   SO 123922

Beside a golf course east of Newtown is a very impressive motte and bailey castle probably built in the 1080s by Roger de Montgomery. The inner bailey 18m wide by 38m long is strongly protected by the steep fall of the ground to the River Severn on the north and east, the 9m high motte with a summit diameter of 11m to the south, and a rampart on the west rising 5m above a ditch 2m deep. An outer bailey 30m wide on the south and 45m wide on the west, where there is a rampart 2m high, protects the outer sides of the motte away from the river.

HEN DOMEN   SJ 241188

This mound in a commanding position has been damaged by badgers. It rises 6m to an irregularly shaped and eroded summit 13m in diameter.

Hen Domen

HEN DOMEN SO 214981 F

This was the original Montgomery Castle recorded in the Shropshire part of the Domesday Book survey of 1086 as being held by Roger de Montgomery, who is thought to have erected it in 1075. Extensive excavations have shown that the fine and numerous timber framed buildings clustered close together in the bailey were rebuilt many times before being finally abandoned c1300. So this site remained in use for over seventy years after the new royal castle of stone was built on the high rock further south. Traces were found of no less than five successive bridges leading directly up from a large hall to the lord's house or tower on the 16m diameter motte summit. The bailey is 50m wide and extends 38m east of the motte ditch. Evidence was found that its palisade had timber flanking towers and a gatehouse of some pretension. A high counterscarp bank surrounds the whole castle except on the south where a modern road has caused its removal. On the west it has its own outer ditch. In c1105 Henry I granted the castle to Baldwin de Bollers and his descendants held it until 1207. It was captured by the Welsh in 1214.

HYSSINGTON CASTLE SO 315945

The small hill SE of the church with a steep slope on the NE side has been formed into a triangular bailey 70m long by 45m wide. The buried base of a tower 9m square on a low mound occupies the north corner and traces have been seen in the east corner of a probably hall-block 18m by 9m externally, plus another building. Ruins of these structures still stood in 1811. this site is perhaps more likely than Symon's Castle 3km to the WSW to be the castle of Snead occupied by Simon de Parcio in 1231, and given by Henry III to William de Bowles in 1233.

KERRY MOTTE SO 147895

The overgrown mound on a hillock south of the village was built by Madog ap Idnerth c1135 to counter the power of the Mortimers. The summit about 10m across rises 7m above the ditch on the NW side where a comma-shaped bailey 38m by 24m lies beyond.

LLANDRINIO MOTTE SJ 294168

On the bank of the River Severn 400m SSW of the church lay a small motte and bailey castle, the remains of which are now engulfed within a modern flood bank.

LLANFECHAIN MOTTE SJ 186202

The mound above the Afon Cain SW of the village is likely to have been built by Owain Fychan ap Madog, who captured Mochnant in 1166. The mound rises 6m above a ditch with a counterscarp bank to a flat summit 12m across. A shovel-shaped bailey 45m long by 35m wide on the NE has a natural slope to the north and east, a ditch to the west, and on the south a rampart rising 2m above a ditch 1m deep.

LLANGADFAN MOTTE SJ 012107

Overlooking the Banwy west of the Cann Office Hotel is a remnant of a motte. The hotel lies on the site of the bailey 34m by 30m with an entrance on the south facing a loop of the river.

LLANIDLOES CASTLE   SN 954844

After Owain de la Pole was granted a charter in 1280 for a market at Llanidloes he laid out the town on a rectangular plan beside the Severn. It was protected by a rampart and ditch on the north and east sides and had gates in the middle of each of the west, north, and east sides, whilst the south side was closed off by a castle of earth and wood. It had a moated mound 30m across on top and 3m high which lay behind the Mount Inn, and to the east, where the Community and Health centres now lie, was an oval bailey 60m long by 50m wide. Streams to the south and east of the town and castle probably filled wet moats.

LLYSLUN MOTTE   SJ 033101

In the 1170s Owain Cyfeiliog gave this castle to Maredudd, the exiled brother of Gruffydd ap Cynan of Gwynedd. A natural hillock with a steep drop on the south side has been scarped into a tiny motte rising 3m above the ditch dividing it from a bailey platform to the west which is 15m long by 12m wide.

LUGGY MOAT   SO 199022

The Luggy Brook has cut a cliff into the north side of the 9m high motte showing that it is composed of layers of rubble levelled with spreads of clay. Because of erosion damage on the south side the summit has now assumed a rectangular shape 16m long by 10m wide. To the east slight scarps delineate a bailey platform 54m north-south by 45m wide.

MANAFAN MOTTE   SJ 114022

The farm probably lies on the site of the bailey of the damaged 9m high motte to the NE with a summit 9m in diameter.

The motte at Mathrafal

MATHRAFAL CASTLE   SJ 131107

Mathrafal was an original capital of the Princes of Powys, ranking alongside Aberffaw and Dinefwr as one of the three royal seats of Wales. The fort on the hill 1km NW may have been the original royal seat, and the ramparts and ditches enclosing a square of about 100m upon flat ground beside the west bank of the Banwy may be of the 10th or 11th century. The motte in the east corner and the small bailey in front of it were built either by Owain Cyfeiliog c1170 or Robert de Vieupont on behalf of King John in 1212 after Gwenwynwyn, son of Owain had transferred his chief seat to Welshpool. The castle was destroyed the same year by Llywelyn ap Iorwerth. Evidence of a retaining wall on the east side of the bailey towards the river were formerly visible.

MON-Y-LLYN MOTTE   SJ 210010

Beside a farm probably set on the site of a bailey is an overgrown motte rising 9m to an oval summit 18m by 15m across. Probably this castle was built in the 1080s by Roger Corbet of Caus Castle.

MOEL FROELAS MOTTE   SJ 118225

Two sections of ditch isolate a motte 6m high with a top 10m across from the rest of a high ridge above the Banwy. The site has steep falls away on each side except to the east where there are traces of a bailey.

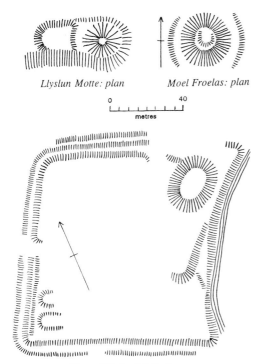

Llyslun Motte: plan   *Moel Froelas: plan*

0   40
metres

Plan of Mathrafal Castle

Middle Ward wall at Montgomery

MONTGOMERY CASTLE   SO 221967   C

The teenage Henry III came with his army to Montgomery in the autumn of 1223 and ordered work begun on a new stone castle on a high rock 2km south of the original wooden Montgomery castle at Hen Domen. By November wooden buildings had been put up and Forest of Dean miners were cutting ditches through the rock. About £2,000 was spent on clearing a field of fire, providing a garrison, and walling the inner ward in 1224-6. The king granted the castle in April 1228 to his justiciar, Hubert de Burgh, Earl of Essex. It withstood attacks by Llywelyn ap Iorwerth during the summers of 1228 and 1231, although the town growing up below the castle was burnt on the latter occasion. Work on an outer court towards the Cedewain road was in hand in 1229. Hubert de Burgh fell from grace in 1232 and the castle was back in royal hands in 1233 when the main tower was roofed in lead.

John le Strange was custodian of the castle in 1240. A new drawbridge, stable and road up to the castle were provided in 1248-51, the middle ward gatehouse was under construction in 1251, and then £50 was spent on replacing the middle ward timber palisade with a stone curtain wall. Henry III was at Montgomery in 1267, signing there a treaty which acknowledged Llywelyn ap Gruffydd as Prince of Wales.

Edward I had the town walled in stone in 1279-80 as part of his contest with Llywelyn ap Gruffydd. In the 1280s over £100 was spent on providing the castle with a new hall, chamber, kitchen, bakehouse, and granary. Montgomery formed part of the dowry of Margaret, Edward's new queen, in 1299, but was transferred to the Prince of Wales in 1301. It was granted to Edward II's widow Queen Isabella in 1327 and in 1330 was granted to Roger Mortimer, Earl of March. He was executed by Edward III later that year and the castle lay neglected and ruinous until granted in 1359 to Roger's grandson and namesake, who became 2nd Earl of March. He rebuilt the Well Tower and repaired the walls of the middle ward.

Inner gateway at Montgomery

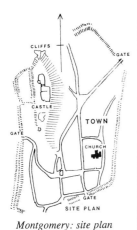

Montgomery: site plan

Montgomery Castle

The castle was little used by the later Earls of March and was left to decay until Rowland Lee, Bishop of Coventry and Lichfield, was made President of the Council of the Marches of Wales in 1534. He regarded the castle at Montgomery as second in importance only to his headquarters at Ludlow Castle. He renovated the domestic buildings and military stores, and the 100 men at work here during the summer of 1538 were probably erecting the ranges of lodgings whose foundations can be seen around three sides of the middle ward.

The Herbert family were associated with Montgomery Castle as early as 1526, when Sir Richard Herbert was custodian for Henry VIII. During Elizabeth I's reign the family had a house called Blackhall in or near the town and a survey of 1593 shows the castle as standing empty and decayed. In 1622 Sir Edward Herbert, created Lord Herbert of Chirbury in 1629 by Charles I, began to build a splendid new timber-framed house in the middle ward. He surrendered the castle to a Parliamentary force led by Sir Hugh Myddelton in September 1644 on condition that the building and its contents were spared. However Lord Herbert died in 1648, and, since his successor Richard was an active Royalist, it was ordered in 1649 that both the new house and the old castle should be demolished. Portions of the buildings, probably the upper part of the inner gatehouse, are said to have fallen in the early 19th century. By the 1960s, when the Earl of Powys handed the site over to the Ministry of Works and excavations were begun, only two fragments stood above the mound of debris which covered most of the walls and ditches.

The castle comprised an inner ward, a middle ward to the south, and a larger outer enclosure beyond that which probably only ever had wooden defences and which now contains a farm. The middle ward is 60m long with a maximum width of 37m. It was defended by ditches to the south and west and had a wall 2m thick with a small round SE corner turret, and other turrets at the NE corner flanking a postern which opened out of the inner ward ditch. On the south was the gatehouse with a passage flanked by rectangular chambers with rounded fronts towards the field. Most of the wall is reduced to foundations and was perhaps lowered in the 1620s when the new Herbert mansion was built inside it. More survives on the east where the ground slope made a greater height of wall necessary. The space behind this wall was filled in by Bishop Lee to level the court for building upon but it is now cleared down to its 13th century level again. Traces of lodgings remain on the west side.

Two solid half-round towers 7m in diameter flank the outer part of a passage through a gatehouse 18m wide which leads to the court 39m long by 22.5m wide of the inner ward. The passageway was closed with a portcullis and two sets of doors and had two recesses with cupboards, possibly for housing lamps. The room east of the passage was for the porter or guard. That to the west was originally a dark prison only entered by a trap-door from above. A doorway was later broken through from the west recess of the passage. Only the west end wall now remains of the upper levels. The hall was reached by a timber stair from the court and according to the 1593 survey had a timber chapel set on posts built against the north side. Above were two further storeys each containing one large room with a latrine in a sidewall. A gallery connected the gatehouse apartments with chambers within the Well Tower, a large U-shaped structure 15m long by 12m wide with a well in its base. Seeping water seems to have caused continual structural problems and most of what remains of the tower outer walls are of c1360. The second storey room in this tower was used as a dining room in 1593. Only foundations remain of the kitchen north of the tower and the offices and lodgings on the north and east sides of the inner ward probably dating from the 1280s. A D-shaped north tower was dismantled in the 1280s or 1360s and only the base still remains. East of it was a postern leading to the northern outworks.

Sections of a rampart and ditch remain around the west and east sides of the town. Part of a round tower remains near the Cottage Inn on the north side and excavations have revealed the base of another at the SW corner. Leland described the stone walls and the Cedewain Gate on the west, the Ceri Gate on the south, the Chirbury Gate on the NE, and Arthur's Gate on the north as decayed in the 1530s.

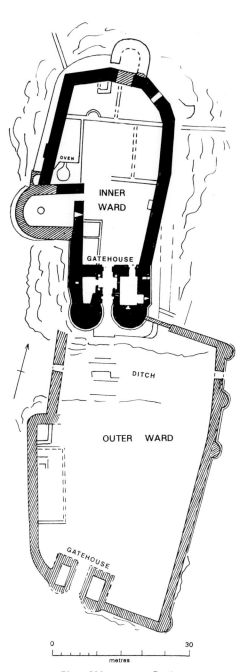

Plan of Montgomery Castle

NANTCRIBBA CASTLE   SJ 237014

Modern quarrying has dramatically increased the extent of natural cliffs on the east side of a wooded hill beside Offa's Dyke. Around the hill is a ditch, still partly water filled, possibly a relic of a Dark Age settlement. On the overgrown summit of the hill are the last traces of a stone wall around a court about 39m by 33m with round towers at the west and south corners. Probably this was the castle of Gwyddrwg begun c1260 by Thomas Corbet of Caus Castle, and destroyed in 1263 by Gruffydd ap Gwenwynwyn, probably never to be restored.

NEWTOWN MOTTE   SO 106915   F

In 1279 Cedewain was granted to Roger Mortimer and in 1280 he was granted a charter for a weekly market which seems to have been at Newtown, which lies within a bend of the River Severn. Probably the weak south side was then provided with a rampart and ditch, and a mound rising 5m above a wide ditch to a summit 39m across was provided in the middle of this side. Possibly an outer enclosure extended westward from the mound to the river bank. The base of a small stone building on the mound summit found in 1910 may have dated from 1641, when the site was refortified by Sir John Price. By then half of the mound had been levelled and he dug a new ditch along the resulting straight side.

NEUADD COCH MOTTE   SO 079878

Hidden in woodland is a promontory above a tributary of the Mochre Brook which has been scarped into a motte 7m high with a top 15m long.

OLD HALL CAMP   SO 207897

On a spur high up to the south of Sarn is a ringwork thought to be the site of a castle begun in 1228 by Hubert de Burgh in an attempt to establish an English domination of Ceri Woods. It was called "Hubert's Folly" since after a few weeks work the fortifications were left incomplete. In the 16th century the site was called Castell Machaethlon. It has a maximum width of 45m with north and south sides curving round to meet at right-angles 60m apart at the east and west, the entrance being at the latter. The ditch is quite formidable on the weak SW side, where there is a rampart, but it was probably left much shallower than intended on the stronger northern sides.

PEN-Y-CASTELL MOTTE   SN 954844

A ringwork 24m across rises 5m above the ground on the south side but just 3m above the worn down bailey 60m across on the north side.

PLAS-YN-DINAS   SJ 218189

A low shelf of land above a loop of the River Vyrnwy has been made into a defensive enclosure measuring about 125m by 105m. Possibly of Dark Age origin, this site was still in use as late as the middle third of the 14th century, when it was held by Thomas ap Rhodri from John de Charlton, Lord of Powys.

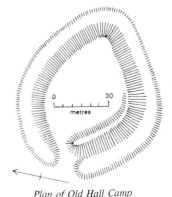

Plan of Old Hall Camp

POWIS CASTLE   SJ 215064   O

In the inner ward of Powis Castle, which is also known as Castell Coch (Red Castle) from the colour of the sandstone of which it is built, the lower parts of a square keep and separate hall block are detectable under all the later building work. Although these might normally be regarded as work of c1200 there are reasons for believing that the chief seat of the Princes of Powys remained at the motte and bailey site by the town of Welshpool until it was destroyed in 1274 by Llywelyn ap Gruffydd because Gruffydd ap Gwenwynwyn had sided with the English. So the keep and hall-block were probably begun after Gruffydd was restored as ruler of Powys by Edward I, and continued after 1286 by his son Owain, who took the English type surname de la Pole (Pole or Pool being the original name of Welshpool). Quite how the 4.5m high motte with a summit diameter of 17m lying on the shelf of land west of Powis Castle fits into the story is uncertain. Perhaps it served as an outwork of the castle at Welshpool.

After Owain died in 1309 the castle passed under English law to his daughter Hawys who married John de Charlton. However under Welsh law her uncle Gruffydd claimed the castle and he besieged her within it unsuccessfully in 1312. Edward, fifth Lord Charlton was blockaded in the castle by his own tenants in support of Owain Glyndwr in 1403, and assistance was sought from Henry IV. When Edward died in 1421 his estates were divided between his daughters. The inner ward of Powis Castle became the residence of Joan and her husband John de Grey and was kept in repair, a substantial gateway tower being added at the north end to give them direct access without going through the outer court. Possession of the outer ward passed eventually to the Suttons, Lords of Dudley Castle in Staffordshire. According to Leland their part of Powis Castle was left to decay.

Powis Castle

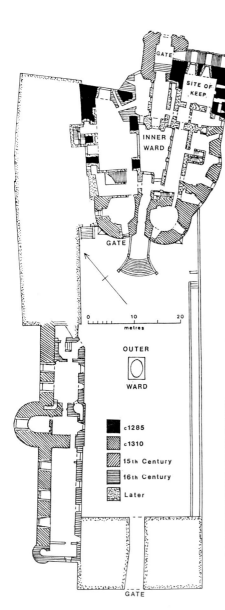

Powis Castle

Powis Castle

Plan of Powis Castle

Powis Castle was re-united under one family in the 16th century and in 1587 was purchased from Grey descendants by Sir Edward Herbert. He immediately began improving the accommodation at the castle and the Long Gallery and numerous windows in the outer walls are relics of this campaign whilst the NW range in the outer ward is probably his replacement or remodelling of a late medieval structure. His son William was created Lord Powis by Charles I in 1629. During the Civil War the castle was a Royalist stronghold until on the 2nd of October 1644 Sir Thomas Myddelton captured it in a surprise night attack, during which his master gunner John Arundell blew up the outer gate. The building then lay ruinous until the 1660s.

The 3rd Lord Powis, who was created an earl in 1674 and a Marquess in 1685, began rebuilding and remodelling which included a new state bedroom. The work continued under William III's nephew William Van Zuylesteyne, Earl of Rochford, who had possession of the castle whilst the Catholic 1st and 2nd Marquesses were in exile after the deposition of James II in 1688. The 2nd Marquess finally returned to the castle in 1722. When the 3rd Marquess died in 1748 Powis went to an heiress who married Henry Herbert, for whom George II revived the earldom of Powis. Their daughter Henrietta married Edward Clive for whom the Powis earldom was revived again in 1804. Part of the Clive fortune was spent on another remodelling of Powis Castle in 1815-18 to designs by Sir Robert Smirke. The 4th Earl of the new creation carried out further work in the early 20th century. His sons died during the two world wars and when he himself died in 1952 the castle was given to the National Trust, although it remains a home of George Herbert, 7th Earl, who is descended from a cousin of the 4th Earl.

The inner ward has only a tiny central court 9m long by 7m wide within which there was formerly a very deep well. The court is reached from the outer ward by a narrow canted passageway with two portcullis grooves. The outer arch and the massive round towers nearly 12m in diameter which flank it are early 14th century but the three storeys of rooms in each tower have three-light mullion-and-transom windows and other features of the 1590s. The thick walled block on the NW side of the court now containing the library and Blue Drawing Room above the Dining Room is likely to be late 13th century work although all the features are of many dates from the late 16th century onwards. The NE tower added by the Greys contained two upper living rooms above a lierne-vaulted gateway until Smirke added a fourth storey. The lower parts of the corner turrets are original. This gateway, now closed, formed the principal entrance to the castle in the late 15th century. It adjoins a late 13th century tower roughly 13m square which formed a keep. The lowest storey has been much altered and the upper storeys were entirely rebuilt with thinner walling in the 1590s when part of one room became the NE end of the Long Gallery occupying the SE range second storey. This range has 16th century windows through the medieval curtain wall but is otherwise mostly of later periods.

The outer ward is 30m wide and extends for 68m to the SW. The SE side is closed by a modern low level wall-walk probably on the footings of a medieval curtain. Original walling 2.8m thick remains to a great height on the NW side together with a D-shaped tower 9m in diameter. The range containing the shop and tea-room set against this wall may have 15th and 16th century masonry but was altered in the 1770s to create a narrow ballroom, south of which is a room now containing the Clive Museum. The SW range contains stables and a coach house flanking the outer gateway passage. Excavations in 1984 by the south corner revealed part of the base of a round tower which flanked the medieval gateway blown up in 1644.

The motte in the park at Powis

RHOS DDIARBED CASTLE   SO 046905

This impressive earthwork was probably built by
Roger de Montgomery in the 1080s. It is a classic
motte and bailey layout on a level site which was
perhaps once marshy, so the ditches may have been
water filled. The 9m high motte with a summit 15m
across stands at the south end of an oval bailey
extending 55m from the outer edge of the motte ditch
to the entrance gap in the 4m high rampart at the
north end. The bailey is about 55m wide. A
farmhouse stands within the much larger but more
feebly defended rectangular outer bailey 180m long
by over 100m wide extending to the north.

RHYD-YR-ONEN CASTLE   SN 923823

A motte 6m high with a summit 15m across lies
across a promontory sloping from south to north
where two streams converge far below. There is a
small enclosure on the tip of the promontory and a
much bigger one 65m wide extending 55m from the
motte ditch to a high rampart on the south. Because
of the slope the rampart, which has an entrance gap
on the east, lies higher than the motte summit.

RHYSNANT MOTTE   SJ 256175

A very mutilated ringwork lies in woodland above
Rhysnant Hall.

Plan of Rhos Ddiarbed Castle

Symon's Castle

SYMON'S CASTLE   SO 285933

A motte 4m high created by cutting a ditch through rock backs onto a south-facing cliff which has been dramatically increased in height by modern quarrying. Excavations in the 1980s revealed footings of the 1.8m thick wall of a shell keep 21m across inside built from stone taken out of the ditch.

TAFOLWERN CASTLE   SH 891026

The low-lying motte between the Afon Twymyn and Afon Rhiw Saeson (which may have been dammed to form moats) was probably the seat of Owain Cyfeiliog, who was granted Cyfeiliog commote in 1149 by his uncle Madog ap Maredudd. When Madog died in 1160 his relatives quarrelled amongst themselves and in the confusion Cyfeiliog was taken over by Owain Gwynedd. The castle was captured in 1162 by Hywell ap Ieuaf, Lord of Arwystli. Owain raided Arwystli, defeated Hywell, and rebuilt the wrecked castle. By 1165 he had returned it to Owain Cyfeiliog, but the latter was expelled from all his lands when he renewed his former allegiance to the Normans. The castle was briefly held by Rhys ap Gruffydd but was recaptured by Owain Cyfeiliog with Norman help. It was occupied by Owain's son Gwenwynwyn in the later 12th century and is last mentioned when Owain's grandson Gruffydd was isolated there in 1244 by a Welsh army because of his support for Henry III, and John le Strange wrote to Henry III asking for his help.

TOMEN CEFN COCH MOTTE   SJ 105263

A mound rising 6m to a summit 11m across with traces of a ditch on the west side lies on a commanding site above the Tanat Valley.

TOMEN-YR-ALLT MOTTE   SJ 126211

A hilltop above the Nant Fyllon 2km from Llanfyllin has been scarped into a motte 15m high with a top 10m across with a 3m deep ditch with a counterscarp and a large bailey to the SE. This is likely to have been the castle of Boyddon captured in 1257 by Llywelyn ap Gruffydd from Gruffydd ap Gwenwynwyn when the latter sided with Henry III.

WELSHPOOL CASTLE   ST 230074   V

The earthwork known as Domen Castell near to Welshpool station may be the castle built in 1111 by Cadwgan ap Bleddyn, newly instated as ruler of Powys. Probably it was this castle that was captured by the English in the 1190s and soon recaptured by Gwenwynwyn. It was still mostly a wooden structure in 1274 when Gruffydd ap Gwenwynwyn plotted against Llywelyn ap Gruffydd and was deposed and his seat at Pool captured and destroyed. The rampart of the oval bailey 60m by 46m has been greatly remodelled for the use of spectators of a bowling green created within it. On the south side is an overgrown motte rising 5m to a summit 9m in diameter.

Plan of Rhyd-Yr-Onen Castle

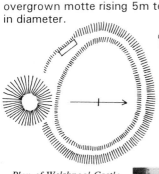

Plan of Welshpool Castle

Cefn Coch: plan

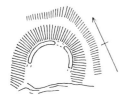

Symon's Castle: plan

Welshpool Castle

GAZETTEER OF CASTLES IN RADNORSHIRE

ABEREDW CASTLE   SO 079473 & 076474   V

The castle at Aberedw visited by Llywelyn ap Gruffydd just before he was killed in a nearby skirmish with English troops in 1282 must have been Hen Castell, a ditched motte with footings of what appears to be a D-shaped tower. It lies SW of the church with a steep drop to a tributary of the Wye on the south and a ditch on the other sides. The other castle site west of the village was fortified by Walter Hakelutel, one of Edmund Mortimer's knights, in accordance with a licence to crenellate granted by Edward I in 1285. It has been abandoned by 1397. A wall 1.8m thick, of which only foundations remain, surrounded a courtyard about 36m square. Part of the inner wall of a range of buildings on the north side can be traced. At the SE corner is the base of a round tower 6m in diameter and there are signs of former towers at the NE and NW corners, the latter being perhaps larger than the others. The SW corner and all of the west wall vanished when this side was cut away for building a railway. The remaining sides have a dry moat 9m wide and over 2m deep.

BARLAND MOTTE   SO 281618

This site has steep falls away on the south and east but was weak since it was overlooked by higher ground to both the north and south. It lies very close to the border with Herefordshire. There are traces of footings of a wall around a court with a ditch on the north side, whilst a farm track passes closeby on the west. The 3m high mound on the south side is actually the buried base of a small square tower keep. The castle may date from the 1160s, when Barland was granted by William de Braose to the Peytevin family, who were still here in 1304, although during the latter part of King John's reign when the de Braose possessions were in royal hands, Barland was held by Simon Cook.

Aberedw Castle

BEDDUGRE CASTLE

SO 101895

On a hill above the west side of the Ithon is the site of what is thought to have been the seat of the princes of Maelienydd. A large D-shaped outer enclosure, perhaps a settlement, lay below and east of a low ditch mound cutting off the neck of a spur and having a ramparted bailey to the south of it, and traces of outworks to the north.

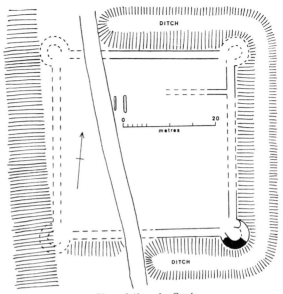

Plan of Aberedw Castle

BLEDDFA CASTLE   SO 209682

The very overgrown motte and small bailey lie SE of the church, beside a stream. In 1195 Hugh de Say was licensed by Richard I to refortify the castle and the square tower of which slight traces remain on top of the motte was probably built around that time, although Hugh himself was killed in the battle of Radnor later the same year. It appears that the top 3m of the 9m high motte is in fact the buried stump of this keep. The castle was destroyed in 1262 after being captured by Llywelyn ap Gruffydd from the Mortimers. In 1304 Edward I allowed material from the destroyed castle to be used to build the church tower, itself destroyed by the Welsh c1403. The bailey has slight traces of two former towers and seems to have been defended by an artificial lake on its west and south sides.

BOUGHROOD CASTLE   SO 132391

The castle was probably built by a younger brother of Cadwallon, Lord of Maelienydd, Einion Clyd, who was murdered in 1140, or his son Walter Fychan, to whom Boughrood was eventually restored by the Bishop of Hereford. It was later held by the Gamage family until Matthew Gamages was dispossessed by King John in 1205. Probably the castle was destroyed in 1215 since there is no mention of it in documents of the 1220s and 30s. The Gamages family eventually got the castle back and it then passed by marriage to the Pembridges. Some time during the mid 13th century the castle was rebuilt only to be destroyed in the 1260s by Llywelyn ap Gruffydd. An excavation was carried out on the mound beside Castle Farm in 1966, with the expectation that the base of a square keep would be revealed, since a tower was mentioned in 1205. However only fragments of mortar and 13th century pottery were discovered, all the stones having been robbed, perhaps in 1800 when Francis Foulke erected a mansion on or near the castle site. The farm lies on the bailey site and its buildings have encroached upon and damaged the motte.

BURFA CASTLE   SO 275611

The 4m high mound seems to have borne a polygonal shell keep about 18m across. On the south side the mound has been damaged by the construction of buildings probably associated with a mill. There are slight traces of what may have been the west and north walls of a small bailey to the north. Burfa was held by Ralph St Ouen in 1304 but the castle may have already been ruinous by then.

CASTELL CAEMARDY   SO 035530

A small motte 3m high lies on a hill 2km north of Builth Wells. It has a ditch on one side and a steep drop away on the other.

CASTELL CRUGERYDD   SO 158593   V

On a commanding spur west of the A44 is a D-shaped bailey platform 47m in diameter by 28m wide rising up to 2m above the surrounding ditch. A motte with its own ditch lies on the straight west side. It rises 4m to a summit 8m in diameter. This castle was visited by Giraldus Cambrensis on his tour of Wales in 1188, and it was probably built in the 1150s by Cadwallon ap Madog. It is likely to derive its name from the herald-bard Llywelyn Crug Eryr, who lived here c1300. The site seems to have still been in use in Owain Glyndwr's day, and according to a 17th century account it was "defaced" by him. An excavation in the 1930s is said to have revealed the bases of walls with doorways but unfortunately no written reports of this have survived.

Castell Gemaron

CASTELL FOEL ALT   SO 258676

In a flat meadow beside the River Lugg below Pilleth Church stands a small motte 7.5m high with slight traces of outer defences. It was probably built by Ralph Mortimer of Wigmore in the 1086 and was still in use in 1341 when a dowager of the Mortimers of Wigmore lived here. The motte seems to have borne a stone tower.

CASTELL GEMARON   SO 153703   V

Alternatively known as Cymaron or Cwm Aran, this castle was probably erected in the 1090s by Ralph Mortimer and continued to serve the Mortimers as an important manorial seat until at least the 1360s. It is first mentioned in 1144 when it was rebuilt by Hugh Mortimer after being captured and destroyed by the Welsh. It is thought to have been captured again by Cadwallon ap Madog c1150. After he died in 1179 the castle was occupied by the Sheriff of Hereford and repaired, but Cadwallon's sons are though to have retaken the castle in 1182. They were expelled by Roger Mortimer in 1195. In 1215 the castle was destroyed by Llywelyn ab Iorwerth, but it was rebuilt again in the 1240s. A farmhouse lies within the eastern half of a quadrangular bailey 60m by 50m with a steep fall to the River Aran on the east, and a rampart and ditch on the other sides. On the south is a large but rather shapeless motte without a flat summit with a rock outcrop forming its core. A counterscarp bank on the SW protects both motte and bailey against the higher ground beyond. Further west is a tributary stream and a 6m high mound, possibly a siege camp. A second possible siege mound stands on the south side of the river.

CASTLE NIMBLE   SO 247594

Beside a stream in a valley below Old Radnor church are what look like a very low motte 18m in diameter and a bailey about 25m square. In fact the earthworks are probably the buried footings of stone walls built on the bedrock. Presumably a combination of wet moats and marshland made the site defensible.

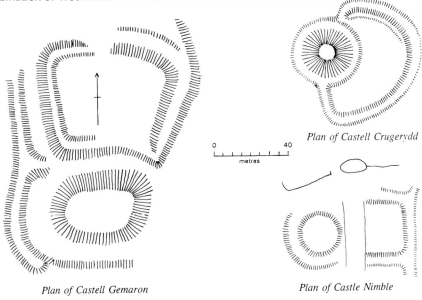

Plan of Castell Crugerydd

0   40
metres

Plan of Castell Gemaron

Plan of Castle Nimble

Cefnllys, looking from the 1273 castle site to the the 1242 castle site

CEFNLLYS CASTLE   SO 088614   F

The strong defensive site known as Castle Bank which is almost surrounded by a wide and deep bend of the Ithon, within which lies the church, was probably occupied during the Iron Age. The original castle of this district was the motte beside the river at Dinieithon, 1.5km NNE of Cefnllys church. The new stone castle begun c1242 by Ralph de Mortimer was on Castle Bank, and it may have been fortified by the Mortimers previous to then. The castle was probably nearly complete by 1246 when Ralph died, leaving only a daughter. His castle appears to have comprised a round keep with an oval bailey 50m long by 40m wide to the west with an outer bailey of similar size at a lower level to the east.

In November 1262 the Welsh of Maelienydd revolted against the Mortimers. At Cefnllys they killed the castle porters, captured the constable, and destroyed the castle. Roger de Mortimer and Humphrey de Bohun brought a force to the district and camped in the ruins but Llywelyn ap Gruffydd besieged them there and they were obliged to accept the offer of a free passage back to their territories east of Offa's Dyke. The Treaty of Montgomery made in 1267 allowed Roger de Mortimer to refortify Cefnllys but the prince and baron disagreed on the interpretation of this. Llywelyn complained to Edward I when in 1273-4 a new castle was built at Cefnllys This was evidently the building which stood at the more cramped SW tip of the long narrow triangular hilltop. There the ground falls away very steeply all around except to the NE, where a deep moat was cut through the rock. The new building comprised a large circular or octagonal tower keep standing in the middle of a courtyard about 35m square with towers at the corners, that to the east containing the entrance. To the SW was an outer court of similar size at a lower level. The older castle 180m away was presumably levelled to the ground and material from it re-used. Edmund Mortimer garrisoned the new castle against Llywelyn in 1282 with 8 horsemen and 20 infantrymen. The market he granted to the men of Maelienydd in 1297 was probably to be held on the central part of the hilltop between the two castle sites. At his death the town here had 25 burgesses, suggesting a total population of over 100 people. The castle was captured during the Welsh revolt of 1294 and required rebuilding afterwards.

The motte at Dineithon

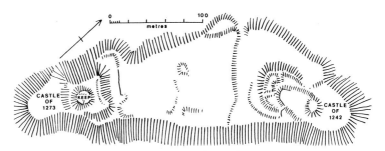

Plan of the castle sites at Cefnllys

Roger Mortimer was obliged to surrender his estates to Edward II in 1322 because of his part in Thomas of Lancaster's rebellion. Maelienydd was granted to the Earl of Kent along with the new castle of Cefnllys, now the capital of the district after the demise of Gemaron Castle. Mortimer only recovered Cefnllys after he deposed Edward II in 1326. Soon after his execution by the young Edward III in 1330 Maelienydd and other confiscated estates were granted to his son Edmund, who died in 1331, leaving Cefnllys to his widow. On her death in 1356 her son Roger repaired the barn, prison, the hall steps and the roof of the keep at Cefnllys.

Edmund Mortimer was a minor during Owain Glyndwr's rebellion and Cefnllys was thus in royal custody. Hugh Burnell was there in charge of 12 spearmen and thirty archers. In 1403 the Bishop and Sheriff of Worcester were ordered to supply them with 8 quarters of wheat, 1 tun of wine, 3 tuns of ale, 200 fish, and 60 quarters of oats. The area around was devastated by the Welsh but the castle itself appears to have remained unharmed.

The vast estates of Edmund Mortimer passed by marriage in 1432 to Richard, Duke of York. He appointed Ieuan ap Philip as constable of Cefnllys Castle. Ieuan's bard Lewis Glyn Cothi wrote a series of poems which have survived. They refer to the rebuilding of the castle hall, and the eight-sided fort which is mentioned may refer to the central tower keep. Cefnllys was merged with the Crown in 1461 when Edward, Duke of York seized the throne. It was granted by Henry VII to his eldest son Arthur in 1493 but probably soon afterwards was abandoned. Camden calls it a ruin in 1558 and the manorial court was transferred to the nearby farm of Neuadd.

CLYRO CASTLE   SO 214436   V

South of a housing estate is a natural hillock which has been made into a large mound up to 40m across on top with a surrounding ditch. There are buried foundations of a polygonal curtain wall probably with a keep or gatehouse on the south side and internal buildings. The castle may have been founded as early as the 1070s as a twin to Hay-on-Wye across the river. At the time when Hay was being refortified in stone Clyro was probably abandoned as its lands had been granted by the princes of Elfael to Abbey Cwmhir. Clyro Castle was probably rebuilt after the Tosny family regained Elfael in 1276, although the first specific mention of the castle is not until the area was being ruled by the Beauchamps from Pain's Castle in 1397. Clyro was amongst the several castles fortified in 1403 against Owain Glyndwr but probably soon fell into decay afterwards.

COLWYN CASTLE   SO 108540

A farm on a hillock above the Edw occupies a ringwork 60m across with a ditch and a counterscarp bank. The ringwork lies within a large rectangular Roman fort. The alternative name of Maud's Castle derives from the wife of William de Braose, by whom the castle is thought to have been built c1196 to replace the castle at Glan Edw. In 1200 King John permitted William Braose to take this district from the Welsh and held it. No ancient stonework survives in situ but mouldings of 13th century type are reset in the farm buildings. The castle seems to have been taken over by King John's forces in 1208 but was captured by the Welsh in 1215. Here in 1232 representatives of Henry III and Llyelyn ab Iorwerth met to discuss the state of the Welsh Border. Sir Owain ap Maredudd ab Einion Clud held Elfael Uwch Mynydd in 1248 and thus presumably the castle, seat of that lordship. Sir Owain was a tenant of Roger Mortimer in July 1260 when he was forced to submit to Llywelyn ap Gruffydd after Builth Castle was captured. Sir Owain and his sons later supported Edward I but rose in revolt late in 1282 and thus lost Colwyn, which passed to Roger Mortimer's widow Maud. The castle is mentioned in 1309 and 1337 but was probably abandoned by 1397 when the Beauchamps ruled Elfael from Pain's Castle.

Dolbedwyn Motte

COURT EVAN GLYNNE   SO 215447

A farmhouse called Castle Kinsey occupies the rectangular bailey platform of an overgrown mound about 4m high which may have borne a stone tower.

DINIEITHON CASTLE   SO 092630

This castle is said to have been built in the 1090s by Ralph Mortimer and to have been destroyed in the 1130s by Madog ab Idnerth. It was the seat of a lordship which took its name from the Welsh commote in which it lay. The castle may have been rebuilt by Madog's son Cadwallon c1165 but is not mentioned after his death in 1179. It was later succeeded by the new castle higher up on a stronger site at Cefnllys. The D-shaped motte rising 5m to a dished summit 18m in diameter lies above the east side of the Ithon 1.5km NNE of Cefnllys church, and guarded a ford. The mound seems to have borne a shell keep and at the beginning of the 20th century traces of a bailey curtain wall also still existed with the footings of an interned gateway.

DOLBEDWYN MOTTE   SO 205491

Above a bend of a tributary of the River Arrow is a tree-covered mound which has collapsed on the south side, where it is 3m high.

DULAS CASTLE   SN 961771

A small ringwork within a marsh is protected by a double moat and rampart system on the west and by streams on the other three sides. The castle was probably built by the Mortimers.

EVANCOYD MOTTE   SO 261632

The 1.5m high mound with a summit 9m across has traces of masonry on the east side, although it seems rather small for a shell keep. This may be the "Newcastle" held as a quarter of a knight's fee by William les Yveteaux in 1211, the lands having probably been separated from Evenjobb just 2km to the south c1180.

EVENJOBB MOTTE   SO 263624

A bungalow stands on the assumed site of a bailey belonging to a mound at the south end. Most of the mound was removed in the 1980s and the rest now forms a rockery but there is a well and evidence of a retaining shell wall about 15m across inside. Not far to the east is a mound 3m high above a bend of the tributary of the River Arrow. The mound seems to be the collapsed remains of a tower, probably round, and it may actually be a mill or water feature of some kind since the supposed bailey to the east has no signs of any defences on the weak northern side. In 1304 Evenjobb was held along with Aston by William Fousel as half a knight's fee.

FFOREST WOOD MOTTE   SO 101529

This is a ditched motte 4.5m high.

Knighton, plan of Bryn Castell

Knighton: the motte at the west end of the town

GLAN EDW CASTLE   SO 116542

At the NW corner of a rectangular embanked enclosure of some size near the River Edw is a motte about 10m high on which are two walls, the last remains of a structure about 18m long by 7.5m wide. The castle was probably built c1093 by Ralph Tosny of Clifford as the new seat of the former Welsh commote of Elfael Uwch Mynydd. It was captured by Madog ab Idnerth c1130, and was rebuilt by Hugh Mortimer in 1144. The Welsh are assumed to have captured it a few years later when Hugh was out of favour with Henry II. The building on the mound may be a relic of the rebuilding of 1195 by William de Braose, but in 1196 the castle was captured and destroyed by Rhys ap Gruffydd. The motte had a wet moat filled from the river which originally came closer to the site. The northern part of the motte has collapsed. There may have been a second courtyard to the north.

GLASBURY   SO 175392

Modern houses and roads now lie on the site of a castle probably erected in 1144 when Walter de Clifford obtained land here from Gloucester Abbey. The last of several Walter Cliffords surrendered the castle to Henry III during the rebellion of 1233 and it was then garrisoned by Henry de Turbeville. It is assumed to have been destroyed by the Welsh in the 1260s and to have not been rebuilt.

GUANCESTE CASTLE   SO 156569

Despite being overlooked by high ground the worn earthworks here commanding a high pass from Elfael into Llythyfnwg seem to have been a small motte with tiny triangular baileys to the north and south of it.

KINNERTON CASTLE   SO 245630

Kinnerton Court, a house of c1700 in the middle of the village, stands in the bailey platform of a 4.5m high motte which seems to have once had a water-filled moat. In the 1250s there was a dispute over the ownership of Kinnerton between Margeria, daughter of Isolda, and William Fitz Elye, who had been granted the land by Roger Mortimer of Wigmore.

Bryn Castell at Knighton

KNIGHTON CASTLE   SO 284722

The overgrown motte in a garden at the west end of the town is probably a relic of a castle erected before 1086 by Hugh L'Asne. A bailey lay between it and the steep fall to the Wylcwm Brook. The motte is 4m high and bears walling of uncertain date and purpose. This castle is mentioned in the Pipe Rolls of 1182, having been taken from Roger Chandos, because he was in rebellion. In 1191 when William de Braose was paid 20 marks in compensation for the government of the absent Richard I having taken over temporary custody of the castle. When William de Braose fell from favour with King John in 1207 the castle was transferred to the custody of Roger Mortimer. He was then ordered to hand the castles of Knighton and Norton over to Thomas Erdington, Sheriff of Shropshire. The rebel William Braose unsuccessfully attacked the castles in 1208, but he later formed an alliance with Llywelyn ab Iorwerth, and both castles were stormed and destroyed in May 1215. Knighton and Norton remained in Welsh hands until in 1230 Llywelyn handed them over as dowry for his daughter on her marriage to Ralph Mortimer. Ralph is assumed to have then refortified the castles of Knighton and Norton in stone. The castle site at Knighton was probably allowed to be enveloped by the growing town after both it and the castle at Norton were destroyed in 1262 by Llywelyn ap Gruffydd. In 1260 the burgesses of the town secured a grant of murage for the construction of town defences, and it appears that the settlement was regarded as defensible in 1402 when Edmund Mortimer sent 400 men from Ludlow to hold it against Owain Glyndwr. No walls survive and a rampart, stockade and ditch may have been considered sufficient as the site is naturally quite strong. Offa's Dyke passes very close to the western edge of the town.

    Bryn Castell, a mound rising 2.5m above a ditch 1m deep to a summit 18m in diameter beside playing fields at SO 290722 east of Knighton, may have been built by Brian Brampton shortly after Knighton was lost to the Welsh in 1215, in which case it would have been abandoned when the Mortimers regained this district in 1230. Rubble on the motte slopes suggests that it may have carried a shell keep.

The earthworks at Pain's Castle

KNUCKLAS CASTLE   SO 250745

On a hilltop high above the village and a tributary of the Teme are the buried footings of a curtain wall around a courtyard about 15m square with round corner towers probably about 6m in diameter. Slightly more survives of the east wall although it is defaced externally and buried internally so no thickness can be determined. On the west is an outer ward or barbican enclosed by high banks. The rest of the hilltop seems to have formed a D-shaped outer court defended by a palisade. The castle is said to have been begun by Ralph Mortimer and completed by his son Roger in 1242. It was destroyed by Llywelyn ap Gruffydd in 1262. It is uncertain whether the remains are of before or after that date, but it is quite likely the site was abandoned after 1262. There is no mention of Knucklas amongst the list of castles belonging to Roger Mortimer which were seized by Edward II in 1322, nor is there any evidence of it being fortified against Owain Glyndwr. In the 1480s Philip ap Howell, who helped Henry VII defeat and replace Richard III, held the manor, but there is no evidence that he made any use of the castle site.

LLANBEDR MOTTE   SO 125449

This tree-clad motte by a track above Bach Howey Brook rises 7.5m from the ditch to a summit 8m across.

LLOWES CASTLE   SO 191407

The motte has recently been eroded by the River Wye, which has destroyed an enclosure beside it and now runs by the south side. The top was made into a military post as part of a training exercise in World War II.

NORTON MOTTE   SO 305673

In the garden of a house is a ditched mound 7.5m high. The site of the bailey has been built over. The site is a hillock above a tributary of the River Lugg. For the history of this Mortimer stronghold see the entry for Knighton.

PAIN'S CASTLE   SO 166462   V

This castle is named after its builder Pain Fitz-John and was probably captured and destroyed by Madog ab Idnerth soon after Pain was killed in July 1137. The castle was rebuilt but soon destroyed again by the Welsh. By the 1190s the castle was held by William de Braose, and his wife Maud is said to have defeated the Welsh at Pain's Castle in 1195. Prince Rhys of Deheubarth besieged the castle in 1196 but failed to take it before a truce was made, and there was another attack in 1198, this time by Gwenwynwyn of Powys, who was incensed by his cousin Talhaiarn having been dragged through Brecon tied to a horse and then beheaded. King John took possession of the castle in 1208 but it was captured in 1215 by the de Braoses' ally Gwalter ab Einion Clud. Gwalter submitted to King John in 1216 and became lord of Elfael, but after he died c1222 the Welsh of that lordship transferred their allegiance to Llywelyn ab Iorwerth, and the castle must have been destroyed around then.

The castle was rebuilt in stone by Henry III in 1231 with a round tower keep on the motte and a curtain wall with an east gatehouse and several D-shaped flanking towers. The castle was granted to Roger Tosny in 1255 and a year after his death in 1264 it was captured and wrecked by the Welsh. Ralph Tosby rebuilt the castle in 1277 and it later passed to the Beauchamps, Earl of Warwick. It was garrisoned by them in 1401 against Owain Glyndwr. Only impressive earthworks remain, comprising a 9m high motte with a summit 22m long, a bailey 60m wide extending 45m north from the motte ditch, and a deep surrounding ditch with a counterscarp bank. On the west side a barbican projects into the ditch from the bailey SW corner.

PENARTH MOTTE   SO 124526

On a spur above the River Edw is a mound rising 5m to a dished top 15m long by 13m wide. There are ditches 1m deep to the NE and SW,

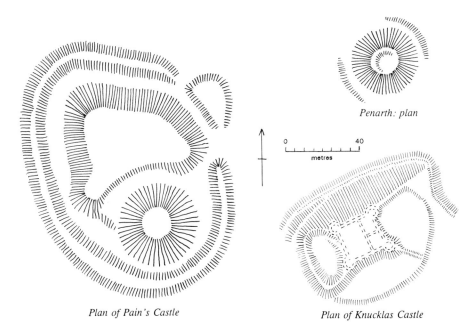

Penarth: plan

0   40

metres

Plan of Pain's Castle

Plan of Knucklas Castle

The town rampart at New Radnor

PRESTEIGNE   SO 310645   F

In a park NW of the town is an oval ringwork about 12m by 24m entered through a bailey of similar size to the east, now rather mutilated. A ditch protects the western side of the ringwork. This castle may have existed by the 1080s and in the 1130s was held by Osbern Fitz Hugh of Richard's Castle. It later passed to the Port family, under whom the Fraxino family held Presteigne. After the Ports were banished in 1172 Presteigne was attached to the sheriffdom of Hereford until purchased by William de Braose in 1203. When he rebelled in 1208 Thomas Fraxino seems to have managed to get the lands of this district made into a barony held directly from King John. However when the de Braose family made their peace with the Crown in 1218 The Fraxinos again became tenants of the barony of Kington. The Mortimers later gained the overlordship through marriage. A charter made by Thomas Fraxino in favour of Wigmore Abbey in 1240 was signed in the hall of Presteigne Castle. In 1262 it was captured and destroyed by the Welsh and probably never restored, since in 1337 the site was recorded merely as "a plot of land called Castle Ditch".

The east end of the great ditch at New Radnor

RADNOR CASTLE   SO 212610   F

The relationship between the castle of New Radnor, the moated site immediately south of Old Radnor Church, and Castle Nimble in the valley north of Old Radnor is uncertain, but it is likely that all the early references to Radnor mean New Radnor, and that Philip de Braose had a stronghold on this fine defensive site by c1095. The site may have been first fortified c1070 by William Fitz Osbern. It was captured by the Welsh in 1182 and taken and destroyed by Rhys ap Gruffydd in 1196 after his victory nearby. The castle was occupied by King John's forces in 1208 after William de Braose was exiled. The king destroyed the castle in 1216, probably after the de Braoses had retaken it. Reginald de Braose rebuilt the castle only for it to be destroyed by Llywelyn ab Iorwerth in 1231. It was rebuilt again, probably in stone, by Henry III's brother Richard, Earl of Cornwall, but was destroyed in 1264 by Llywelyn ap Gruffydd. Rebuilt by Roger Mortimer, the castle was garrisoned against the Welsh in 1282. The many headless skeletons and a separate pile of skulls discovered in 1845, when foundations trenches were dug for the church, must be relics of either prisoners executed after the battle of 1196 or of a luckless 13th century garrison. Henry IV spent nearly £900 on garrisoning the castle from 1402 until 1405 when Richard Grey of Codnor was installed here with a grant of the profits of the surrounding lordships, and fines and ransoms to maintain an adequate garrison. The castle was later left to decay and in 1535 Bishop Roland Lee reported to Thomas Cromwell that the only building worth repairing was the county prison. This was evidently the gatehouse as Leland refers to that part as having been recently repaired.

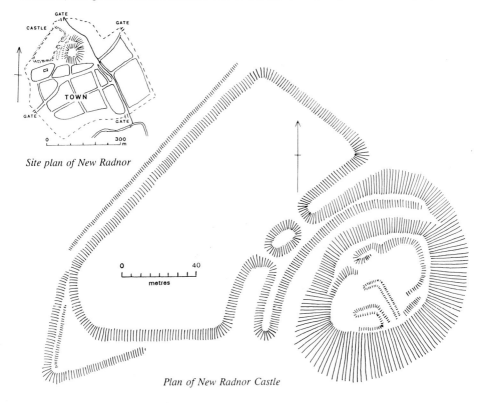

Site plan of New Radnor

Plan of New Radnor Castle

The Earl of Pembroke was nominal constable of Radnor Castle in James I's reign, and Lord Powis in 1631. The castle was able to briefly accommodate Prince Charles in 1642 but soon afterwards it was captured and dismantled by Parliamentary forces. Small cannon balls used in the siege were discovered in the 1780s, and one larger ball was embedded in a wall. In 1815 Thomas Rees recorded the castle as being nearly square with massive towers at the north, east, and NW corners, with two smaller round towers towards the town. However, it is likely he was describing what appears on Speed's map of 1610 rather than observed remains. Pointed arches and foundations were revealed by digging in 1773, 1818 and 1864, the well being discovered on the latter occasion. There were still standing walls in 1840 but only earthworks now remain. The oval inner ward 58m long by 35m wide overlooks a steep drop to the High Street on the south and to the Dingle Brook on the east. To the north and west it is separated from a large outer ward 150m long by 60m wide by a formidable system of two wide and deep dry ditches. The outer ditch may be an addition in connection with the rebuilding of the 1230s, when an outer wall may have been built between the two ditches to strengthen this weaker side. Footings can still be traced of the NE tower, which seems to have been D-shaped, and it is assumed there was a square gatehouse at the NW corner, whilst Speed shows a postern next to the SW tower. The low rampart along the long exposed NW side of the outer ward is actually the buried base of a wall 1.8m thick.

Roger Mortimer obtained a murage grant for walling in the town in 1257, and further grants were made in 1280, 1283 and 1290. From the SW corner of the outer ward of the castle a rampart extends almost as far as the Summergil Brook, which probably fed a wet moat on the south side, and then along to the site of the south gate. South of the site of the west gate shale walling is visible in the bank. Less survives of the eastern section of the defences, where there was a third gate, and the NW section, with a fourth gate near the Dingle Brook. The defences were probably never restored after the destruction wrought in 1403 from which the town never recovered. It only attained the status of county town for Radnorshire in 1536 because of the castle being used as a prison, and it soon lost that status to Presteigne.

Tinboeth Castle

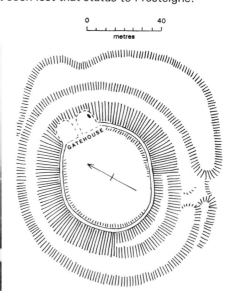

Plan of Tinboeth Castle

0   40
metres

The outer ward at New Radnor

RHAYADER CASTLE   SN 967678 & 968680

The castle built by Rhys ap Gruffydd in 1177 was burnt c1190. Rhys rebuilt it but it was again destroyed in 1195 by Maelgwn and Hywel ap Cadwallon. The damaged motte shows signs of having been revetted and may have supported a tower. In the 18th century it was still known as Tower Hill, and it is said to have been garrisoned in the 1640s. The rectangular bailey site now forms gardens.

The castle site on the east side of the bend of the River Wye with the NE and SE sides defended by a rock-cut ditch containing a spring and having a narrow entrance causeway left at the NE corner is thought to have been fortified c1200 by Roger Mortimer. Almost immediately it was besieged by the Welsh, and after a fortnight the garrison were allowed to leave, and the site was probably never used again. Most of the ditch was later filled in with rubbish.

STANAGE CASTLE   SO 331731

West of Stanage Park is a damaged motte 7m high with a triangular bailey platform to the east. Until 1215 the overlords of Stanage were the Says of Richard's Castle.

TINBOETH CASTLE   SO 090755   F

Also known as Castell Dinbaud, after Maud, widow of Roger Mortimer, this castle lies at 400m on a commanding hill high above the River Irthon and a tributary to the south. It comprises a platform about 40m across surrounded by a rock-cut ditch as much as 9m deep in places with a counterscarp that on the east side extends into an elliptical outer platform 16m wide. A stone curtain wall was built c1275-82, perhaps to replace a palisade destroyed by the Welsh in the 1260s, although there is a possibility that Tinboeth was an entirely new castles of the 1270s and that until then the stronghold of this district was at Castell y Blaidd (Castle of the Wolf) an earthwork of uncertain date lying to the NW across the Ithon at SO 125798. Of the curtain at Tinboeth only buried footings now remain together with several fallen fragments and one standing fragment of what is assumed to have been a typical Edwardian gatehouse with twin round-fronted towers. There are no signs of any other towers or of any internal buildings. The castle was garrisoned against the Welsh in 1282 and was taken from the Mortimers in 1322 but must have been allowed to decay from then on as the exposed site made it unsuitable as a residence.

Tinboeth Castle

TOMEN MOTTE   SO 173589

This motte on a spur north of the A44 is thought to have been held by a junior branch of the princes of Maelienydd in support of the de Braose family. It was probably the seat of Meurig Barach, who was hanged at Bridgnorth by King John in 1212 along with Hywell ap Cadwallon and Madog ap Maelgwn for killing William Moid, and if so would have probably been burnt at that time.

TREWERN CASTLE   SO 132391

This castle may have been built to replace that at Boughrood destroyed c1215, only to be abandoned after a short while, probably because Boughrood was rebuilt. A platform 27m by 9m with steep drops on three sides down to the River Howey is protected on the weak south side by a rock-cut ditch 3.5m deep and 12m wide.

TWYN Y GARTH   SO 108437

On the summit of an isolated hill over 320m above sea level is a weak ringwork 37m across with a rectangular bailey of about the same size to the south. The German World War I field gun west of the ringwork seems to have been there since the 1930s and the site bears signs of army training earthworks dug in 1944.

WOMASTON CASTLE   SO 268606

On a low-lying site by the Summergill Brook and within the grounds of Womaston School stands a 3m high mound with a wet moat. The motte seems to have been revetted by a polygonal shell wall 1.8m thick. The bank close to the north seems to cover the footings of a curtain wall and a well is marked on old maps west of the motte ditch. This castle seems to have been held by the St Ouen family during the 13th century in conjunction with that of Burfa less than 2km to the east.

MOATED SITES IN MID WALES

Several moated sites lie either side of the A470 from Brecon to Hay-on-Wye. That at SO 076321 has a dry shallow ditch 8m wide around a platform 32m long by 24m wide. The platform 29m square at 100336 had a much wider moat fed by the Dulas Brook with outer banks. The sites at 113346, 119326, and 150365 were of similar size, the last of these being much damaged. The larger moat which once enclosed a rectory at 143348 beside Bronllys Church is filled in on the east and NE but still contains water on the south side. These sites are probably all of the 14th century.

In Montgomeryshire there is a large quadrangular enclosure with signs of an outer court at SJ 277129, beside Old Mills Farm. There are smaller quadrangular sites at SO 285958, near Old Church Stoke, SO 094983, below the drive to Gregynog House, SJ 222113, by a house at Guilsfield, and another possible former rectory site at Meifod, at SJ 222113, north of the church, where two streams converge.

Radnorshire has a quadrangular moat at SO 225445, near Hay, and a larger example possibly of Dark Age origin at SO 026532, beside Builth Road Station. The platform at SO 250590 by Old Radnor Church has a deep ditch but is commanded by higher ground to the south. It is likely to be the site of another rectory. The church tower at Old Radnor, probably built soon after a burning of the church by Owain Glyndwr in 1401, commands a considerable view to the north and west. It has arrow-loops in the parapet and does not communicate directly with the church, the doorway (with a drawbar slot) being on the south side. A plan and photograph of this church appear in The Old Parish Churches of Mid Wales (see book list inside back cover).

Moat at Old Radnor

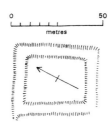

0   50
metres

Talachddu Moat

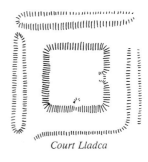

Court Lladca

Moated platform beside Old Radnor Church

A GLOSSARY OF TERMS

BAILEY - Defensible court enclosed by a stone wall or a palisade and ditch. BARBICAN - Defensible court, passage, or porch in front of an entrance. BATTER - The inward inclination of a wall face. BATTLEMENT - A parapet with crenellations. CRENELS - Indentations between the merlons (upstanding portions) of a parapet. CURTAIN WALL - A high enclosing stone wall around a bailey. JAMB - A side of a doorway, window or other opening. KEEP - A citadel or ultimate strongpoint. The term is not medieval and such towers were then called donjons, from which word is derived the word dungeon meaning a prison. LIGHT - A compartment of a window. LOOP - A narrow opening to admit light or for the discharge of missiles. MOAT - A ditch, wet or dry, around an enclosure or bailey. MOTTE - A steep sided flat-topped mound, partly or wholly man-made, upon which the lord's house or tower was sited. MULLION - A vertical member dividing the lights of a window. PARAPET - A wall for protection at any sudden drop. PLINTH - The battered or stepped projecting base of a wall. RINGWORK - An embanked enclosure usually of more modest size than a bailey, generally of rather greater width but less elevated than a motte summit. ROLL-MOULDING - Moulding of semi-circular or D-shaped section. SHELL KEEP - A small stone walled court built upon the summit of a motte or ringwork. SOLAR - A private living room for the lord and his family. TRANSOM - Horizontal member dividing top and bottom lights of a window. WALL-WALK A walkway on top of a wall, protected by a parapet. WARD - A stone walled defensive enclosure.

PUBLIC ACCESS TO THE SITES Codes used in the gazetteers.

C Buildings in the care of Cadw, fee payable at Tretower, otherwise free.
F Other sites to which there is normally free access at any time.
H Buildings currently used as hotels, restaurants, shops (free access to outside).
O Buildings opened to the public by private owners, local councils, National Trust.
V Buildings closely visible from public roads, paths, churchyards & open spaces.

Talgarth Tower

FURTHER READING

Castles of Radnorshire, Paul Remfry, 1996
Castles of Breconshire, Paul Remfry, 1999
The Towns of Medieval Wales, Ian Soulsby, 1983
Castles of the Welsh Princes, Paul R. Davis, 1988
Powys (Buildings of Wales series), Richard Haslam, 1979
Guide pamphlets are available for Powis, Montgomery and Tretower
A History of the County of Brecknock, 4 vols, Theophilus Jones, 1909
Periodicals: Montgomeryshire Collections, Radnorshire Society Transactions, Brycheiniog, Medieval Archeology, Archeolgia Cambrensis.